United States Department of Agriculture

GROWING VEGETABLES
IN THE HOME GARDEN

Prepared by Robert E. Wester

Horticulturist, Northeastern Region,
Agricultural Research Service

Dover Publications, Inc., New York

Published in Canada by General Publishing Company, Ltd.,
30 Lesmill Road, Don Mills, Toronto, Ontario.
Published in the United Kingdom by Constable and Company, Ltd.,
10 Orange Street, London WC 2.

This Dover edition, first published in 1975, is an unabridged republication of the work originally published
in 1972 by the United States Government Printing Office
as U. S. Department of Agriculture *Home and Garden
Bulletin No. 202.*

International Standard Book Number: 0-486-23167-4
Library of Congress Catalog Card Number: 74-28534

Manufactured in the United States of America
Dover Publications, Inc.
180 Varick Street
New York, N.Y. 10014

CONTENTS

page

Selecting a Site 1

Preparing the Soil 4

Choosing Garden Tools 14

Arranging the Garden 17

Selecting Seed 20

Starting the Plants 25

Planting the Garden 39

Caring for the Garden 53

Growing Specific Vegetables 56

State Agricultural Experiment Stations 122

Index of Vegetables 123

PREFACE

This publication is intended for country-wide distribution. Any gardener using it also needs local information, especially on the earliest and latest safe planting dates for vegetables and any special garden practices and varieties that are best for his location. Gardeners may get local information and advice from their state agricultural experiment stations (see page 122) and county agricultural agents.

For single free copies of U.S. Department of Agriculture publications referred to in this book, see your county agricultural agent or write the Office of Communication, U.S. Department of Agriculture, Washington, D.C. 20250.

SELECTING A SITE

A back yard or some other plot near your home in full sunlight is the most convenient spot for a home vegetable garden. However, poor drainage, shallow soil, and shade from buildings or trees may mean the garden must be located in an area farther from the house.

In planning your garden, consider what and how much you will plant. It is better to have a small garden well maintained than a large one neglected and full of weeds. Diagram the garden rows on paper and note the length you wish to assign to each vegetable. Use a scale of a selected number of feet to an inch. Then you can decide how much seed and how many plants to buy.

Consider also the possibility of working your vegetables in plots in front of your shrubbery. Many vegetables are ornamental in appearance. Some vegetables can be grown in your flower beds; others can be grown entirely in containers.

The amount of sunlight your garden gets must also be considered. Leafy vegetables, for example, can be grown in partial shade but vegetables producing fruit must be grown in direct sunlight.

Protecting the Garden

Usually, the garden should be surrounded by a fence sufficiently high and close-woven to keep out dogs, rabbits, and other animals. The damage done by stray animals during a season or two can equal the cost of a fence. A fence also can serve as a trellis for beans, peas, tomatoes, and other crops that need support. In most sections of the country, rodents of various kinds damage garden crops. In the East, moles and mice cause much injury. Moles burrow under the plants, causing the soil to dry out around the roots. Mice either work independently or follow the burrows made by moles, destroying newly planted seeds and young plants. In the West, ground squirrels and prairie dogs damage vegetable gardens. Most of these pests can be partially controlled with traps.

Soil, Drainage, and Sunshine

Fertile, deep, friable, well-drained soil is necessary for a successful garden. The exact type of soil is not so important as that it be well drained, well supplied with organic matter, retentive of moisture, and reasonably free of stones. The kind of subsoil also is vitally important. Hard shale, rock ledges, gravel beds, very deep sand, or a hardpan under the surface soil is likely to make the development of high-grade garden soil extremely difficult or impossible. On the other hand, infertile soil that has good physical properties can be made productive by using organic matter, lime, commercial fertilizer, and other soil improving materials.

Good drainage of the soil is essential. Soil drainage may often be improved by installing agricultural tile, digging ditches, and sometimes by plowing deep into the subsoil. The garden should be free of low places where water might stand after a heavy rain. Water from surrounding land should not drain into the garden, and there should be no danger of flooding by overflow from nearby streams.

Good air drainage is necessary to lessen the danger of damage by frost. A garden on a slope that has free movement of air to lower levels is most likely to escape late-spring and early-autumn frost damage.

A gentle slope of not more than 1½ percent facing in a southerly direction helps early crops get started. In sections that have strong winds, a windbreak of board fence, hedge, or trees on the windward side of the garden is recommended. Hedges and other living windbreaks should be far enough away from the garden to prevent shade or roots from interferring with the garden crops.

The garden should get the direct rays of the sun all day if possible. Some crops can tolerate partial shade, but no amount of fertilizer, water, or care can replace needed sunshine. Even where trees do not shade garden crops, tree roots may penetrate far into the soil and rob crops of moisture and plant food.

Damage to garden crops by tree roots may be largely prevented by digging a trench 1½ to 2 feet deep between the trees and the garden, cutting all the tree roots that cross the trench. Then put a barrier of waste sheet metal or heavy roofing paper along one wall of the trench and refill it. This usually prevents root damage for several years.

PREPARING THE SOIL

Good soil for growing vegetables must be protected by proper cultivation, use of organic matter, maintenance of soil fertility, and control of plant pests. Properly prepared soil provides a desirable medium for root development, absorbs water and air rapidly, and usually does not crust badly.

Tillage practices do not automatically create good garden soil. Tillage is needed to control weeds, mix mulch or crop residues into the soil, and to alter soil structure. Unnecessary tillage increases crusting on the soil surface, and if the soil is wet, tillage compacts it.

Fertility requirements differ between long and short growing seasons and among soil types. In almost every State, the Extension Service will test soils and provide fertilizer recommendations.

Plant pests compete with garden crops and impair their growth. These pests include weeds, insects, fungi, bacteria, viruses, and nematodes. They must be controlled or the garden will not succeed. However, chemical controls must be used carefully to prevent damage to neighboring crops or subsequent crops. When mechanical and chemical controls do not work, crops that are resistant to the pests should be planted in the area for a season or two.

The time and method of preparing the garden for planting depend on the type of soil and the location. Heavy clay soils in the northern sections are frequently benefited by fall plowing and exposure to freezing and thawing during the winter, but when the garden is cover-cropped, it should not be plowed until early spring. In general, garden soils should be cover-cropped during the winter to control erosion and to add organic matter. Gardens in the dry-land areas should be plowed and left rough in the fall, so that the soil will absorb and retain moisture that falls during the winter. Sandy soils, as a rule, should be cover-cropped, then spring-plowed. Whenever there is a heavy sod or growth of cover crop, the land should be plowed well in advance of planting and the soil disked several times to aid in the decay and incorporation of the material. Land receiving applications of coarse manure either before or after plowing should have the same treatment.

Soils should not be plowed or worked while wet unless the work will certainly be followed by severe freezing weather. Sandy soils and those containing high proportions of organic matter—peats and mucks for example—bear plowing and working at higher moisture content than do heavy clay soils. The usual test is to squeeze together a handful of soil. If it sticks together in a ball and does not readily crumble under slight pressure by the thumb and finger, it is too wet for plowing or working. When examining soil to determine if it is dry enough to work, samples should be taken both at and a few inches below the surface. The surface may be dry enough, but the lower layers too wet, for working. Soil that sticks to the plow or to other tools is usually too wet. A shiny, unbroken surface of the turned furrow is another indication of a dangerously wet soil condition.

Fall-plowed land should be left rough until spring, when it may be prepared by disking, harrowing, or other methods. Spring-plowed land should be worked into a suitable seedbed immediately after plowing. Seeds germinate and plants grow more readily on a reasonably fine, well-prepared soil than on a coarse, lumpy one, and thorough preparation greatly reduces the work of planting and caring for the crops. It is possible, however, to overdo the preparation of some heavy soils. They should be brought to a somewhat granular rather than a powdery-fine condition for planting. Spading instead of plowing is sometimes advisable in preparing small areas, such as beds for extra-early crops of lettuce, onions, beets, and carrots.

Organic Matter

Organic matter improves soil as a growing medium for plants. It helps release nitrogen, minerals, and other nutrients for plant use when it decays. A mulch of partially rotted straw, compost, or undecomposed crop residue on the soil helps keep the soil surface from crusting, retards water loss from the soil, and keeps weeds from growing.

Practically any plant material can be composted for use in the garden. Leaves, old sod, lawn clippings, straw, and plant refuse from the garden or kitchen can be used. Often, leaves can be obtained from neighbors who do not use them or from street sweepings.

The purpose of composting plant refuse or debris is to decay it so that it can be easily worked into the soil and will not be unsightly when used in the garden. Composting material should be kept moist and supplied with commercial fertilizer, particularly nitrogen, to make it decay faster and more thoroughly.

The usual practice in building a compost pile is to accumulate the organic material in some

PN-2610

Figure 1.—Making a new compost pile.

out-of-the-way place in the garden. It can be built on open ground or in a bin made of cinder blocks, rough boards, or wire fence. The sides of the bin should not be airtight or watertight. A convenient time to make a compost pile is in the fall when leaves are plentiful (fig. 1.).

In building the compost pile, spread out a layer of plant refuse about 6 inches deep and add one-half pound or one cupful of 10-10-10, 10-20-10, or 10-6-4 fertilizer to each 10 square feet of surface. Then add 1 inch of soil and enough water to moisten but not to soak it. This process is repeated until the pile is 4 to 5 feet high. Make the top of the pile concave to catch rainwater.

If alkaline compost is wanted, ground limestone can be spread in the pile at the same rate as the fertilizer.

The compost pile will not decay rapidly until the weather warms up in spring and summer. In midsummer, decay can be hastened by forking over the pile so moisture can get to parts that have remained dry. The compost should be ready for use by the end of the first summer (fig. 2).

For a continuing supply of compost, a new pile should be built every year. Compost can be used as a mulch, or worked into flower beds and the vegetable garden. (fig. 3).

When properly prepared and thoroughly decayed, compost is not likely to harbor diseases or insects. If the compost is used in soil where an attempt is made to control plant diseases, or if it is mixed with soil used for raising seedlings, the soil should be disinfected with chemicals recommended by your county agricultural agent or State agricultural college.

Commercial Fertilizers

Commercial fertilizers may be used to advantage in most farm gardens, the composition and rate of application depending on locality,

PN-2611

Figure 2.—Compost ready for use in the garden.

PN-2612

Figure 3.—Using a soil-compost mixture under and
around plants in the garden.

soil, and crops to be grown. On some soils with natural high fertility only nitrogen or compost may be needed. The use of fertilizers that also contain small amounts of copper, zinc, manganese, and other minor soil elements is necessary only in districts known to be deficient in those elements. State experiment station recommendations should be followed. Leafy crops, such as spinach, cabbage, kale, and lettuce, which often require more nitrogen than other garden crops, may be stimulated by side dressings. As a rule, the tuber and root crops, including potatoes, sweetpotatoes, beets, carrots, turnips, and parsnips, need a higher percentage of potash than other vegetables.

The quantity of fertilizer to use depends on the natural fertility of the soil, the amounts of organic matter and fertilizer used in recent years, and the crops being grown. Tomatoes and beans, for example, normally require only moderate amounts of fertilizer, especially nitrogen; whereas onions, celery, lettuce, the root crops, and potatoes respond profitably to relatively large applications. In some cases, 300 pounds of commercial fertilizer may be sufficient on a half-acre garden; in other cases, as much as 1,000 to 1,200 pounds can be used to advantage.

Commercial fertilizers, as a rule, should be applied either a few days before planting or when the crops are planted. A good practice is to plow the land, spread the fertilizer from a pail or with a fertilizer distributor, then harrow the soil two or three times to get it in proper condition and at the same time mix the fertilizer with it. If the soil is left extremely rough by the plow, it should be harrowed once, lightly, before fertilizing. For row crops, like potatoes and sweetpotatoes, the fertilizer may be scattered in the rows, taking care to mix it thoroughly with the soil before the seed is dropped, or, in the case of sweetpotatoes, before the ridges are thrown up.

Application of the fertilizer in furrows along each side of the row at planting time does away with the danger of injury to seeds and plants that is likely to follow direct application of the material under the row. The fertilizer should be placed so that it will lie 2 to 3 inches to one side of the seed and at about the same level as, or a little lower than, the seed.

The roots of most garden crops spread to considerable distances, reaching throughout the surface soil. Fertilizer applied to the entire area, therefore, will be reached by the plants, but not always to best advantage. Placing fertilizer too near seedlings or young plants is likely to cause burning of the roots. The fertilizer should be sown alongside the rows and cultivated into the topsoil, taking care to keep it off the leaves so far as practicable.

Heavy yields of top-quality vegetables cannot be obtained without an abundance of available plant food in the soil. However, failure to bear fruit and even injury to the plants may result from the use of too much plant nutrient, particularly chemical fertilizers, or from an unbalanced nutrient condition in the soil. Because of the small quantities of fertilizer required for short rows and small plots it is easy to apply too much fertilizer. The chemical fertilizers to be applied should always be weighed or measured. Table 1 shows how much fertilizer to apply to each 50 or 100 feet of garden row or to each 100 to 2,000 square feet of garden area.

TABLE 1.—*Approximate rates of fertilizer application per 50 or 100 feet of garden row, and per 100 to 2,000 square feet of garden area, corresponding to given rates per acre.*

Measurement	Weight of fertilizer to apply when the weight to be applied per acre is—			
	100 pounds	400 pounds	800 pounds	1,200 pounds
Space between rows, and row length (feet):	*Pounds*	*Pounds*	*Pounds*	*Pounds*
2 wide, 50 long	0.25	1.0	2.0	3.0
2 wide, 100 long	.50	2.0	4.0	6.0
2½ wide, 50 long	.30	1.2	2.4	3.6
2½ wide, 100 long	.60	2.4	4.8	7.2
3 wide, 50 long	.35	1.4	2.8	4.2
3 wide, 100 long	.70	2.8	5.6	8.4
Area (square feet):				
100	.25	1.0	2.0	3.0
500	1.25	5.0	10.0	15.0
1,000	2.50	10.0	20.0	30.0
1,500	3.75	15.0	30.0	45.0
2,000	5.00	20.0	40.0	60.0

If it is more convenient to measure the material than to weigh it, pounds of common garden fertilizer, ammonium phosphate, or muriate of potash, may be converted roughly to pints or cups by allowing 1 pint, or 2 kitchen measuring cups, to a pound. For example, table 1 gives 0.25 pound for a 100-pound-per-acre application to 100 square feet. This would call for about ¼ pint, or ½ cup, of fertilizer. Ground limestone weighs about 1⅓ times as much as the same volume of water; therefore, measured quantities of this material should be about one-fourth less than those calculated as equivalent to the weights in the table. For example, ¾ pint of ground limestone weighs about 1 pound. Ammonium sulfate and granular ammonium nitrate are much lighter, weighing about seven-tenths as much as the same volumes of water; therefore, volumes of these substances calculated by the foregoing method should be increased by about one-third.

Liming

Lime, ground limestone, marl, or ground oyster-shells on garden soils serves a threefold purpose: (1) To supply calcium and other plant nutrients; (2) to reduce soil acidity; (3) to improve the physical character of certain heavy soils. As a rule, asparagus, celery, beets, spinach, and carrots are benefited by moderate applications of lime, especially on soils that are naturally deficient in calcium. Dolomitic limestone should be used on soils deficient in magnesium. Most garden vegetables do best on soils that are slightly acid and may be injured by the application of lime in excess of their requirements. For this reason lime should be applied only when tests show it to be necessary. In no case should the material be applied in larger quantities than the test indicates. Most garden soils that are in a high state of fertility do not require the addition of lime.

With good drainage, plenty of organic matter in the soil, and the moderate use of commercial fertilizers, the growth requirements of nearly all vegetables may be fully met. The local garden leader, county agent, or State experiment station can supply information on soil tests that can be made for each locality. (Samples of soil should not be sent to the U.S. Department of Agriculture.)

Lime, when needed, is spread after plowing and is well mixed with the topsoil by harrowing, disking, or cultivating. Burned lime or hydrated lime should not be applied at the same time as commercial fertilizers or mixed with them, because loss of nitrogen is likely to result, thus destroying part of the plant nutrient value. As a rule, lime should be applied in the spring, because some of it may be washed from the soil during winter. Any of the various forms of lime, such as hydrated and air-slacked lime, may be used but the unburned, finely ground, dolomitic limestone is best. Fifty-six pounds of burned lime or 74 pounds of hydrated lime is equivalent to 100 pounds of ground limestone. Finely ground oystershells and marl are frequently used as substitutes for limestone. Lime should not be used on land that is being planted to potatoes unless the soil is extremely acid, because very low soil acidity increases the development of potato scab.

CHOOSING GARDEN TOOLS

Very few tools are necessary for a small garden. It is better to buy a few simple, high-grade tools that will serve well for many years than equipment that is poorly designed or made of cheap or low-grade materials that will not last. In most instances, the only tools needed are a spade or spading fork, a steel bow rake, a 7-

inch common hoe, a strong cord for laying off rows, a wheelbarrow, and a garden hose long enough to water all parts of the garden. A trowel can be useful in transplanting, but it is not essential. If the soil is properly prepared, plants can be set more easily with the hands alone than with a trowel.

For gardens that are from 2,000 to 4,000 square feet, a wheel hoe is very useful because it can be used for most work usually done with a common hoe and with much less effort. The single-wheel type is probably the easiest to handle and best for use as an all-purpose wheel hoe. Other styles are available and may be used if preferred.

The cultivating tools, or attachments, for the wheel hoe should include one or more of the so-called hoe blades. They are best for weeding and are used more than the cultivator teeth or small plow usually supplied with a wheel hoe.

For gardens over 4,000 square feet, a rotary garden tiller is useful in preparing the soil for planting and controlling weeds.

Many gardeners who do little or no farming have the choice of hiring equipment for garden-land preparation or buying their own. Equipment for hire too often is unavailable when needed, so that a favorable season for planting may be missed. Country gardeners, in increasing numbers, are turning to small farm and garden tractors for land preparation, cultivation, lawn mowing, and hauling sprayers in gardens and orchards. Those who garden every year and who have large homesteads usually find this equipment a good investment. The size and type of equipment needed depend on the amount of work to be done, the contour of the land, and the character of the soil. For cultivating and other light work a 2- to 3-horsepower tractor is used. If plowing or other heavy work is involved, a larger tractor is desirable. Modern outfits of this size are well adapted to cultivating small areas. A medium-size tractor suitable for cultivating a large garden can also be used for plowing.

The rotary tiller, which is capable of preparing light to medium soils for planting in one operation, has been widely adopted by gardeners who have such soils. In the hands of a careful operator and on land that is not too hard and heavy and is reasonably free from stones, roots, and other obstructions, this machine has many desirable features. It can be adjusted to cultivate very shallowly or to plow the soil and fit it for planting. Tools such as sweeps may be attached, thereby adapting the machine to straddle-row cultivating.

Use of well-adapted implements in preparing garden land greatly lessens the work required in cultivating. Clean, sharp, high-grade tools greatly lessen garden labor. For larger gardens, a wheel-type hand fertilizer distributor, a sprayer or duster (preferably a wheelbarrow-type power sprayer), and a seed drill are generally profitable. Minor tools include two pointed iron stakes and weeders.

If sufficient water is available, irrigation equipment is necessary in many areas and highly desirable in nearly all gardens. Furrow application requires careful planning and laying out of the garden area and precise handling of the soil to insure even distribution of water.

Overhead pipes with nozzles at short intervals, temporary lines of lightweight pipe with rotating sprinklers, and porous hose laid along the rows are extensively used. The most common practice is to use a length or two of garden hose, with or without sprinklers, fed by faucets on temporary or permanent lines of pipe through the garden.

In winter, when there is little heat from the sun, little water is used by plants so irrigation is not needed in most areas. However, in summer, rainfall is usually inadequate and irrigation is essential for maximum production.

ARRANGING THE GARDEN

No one plan or arrangement for a garden can suit all conditions. Each gardener must plan to meet his own problem. Careful planning will lessen the work of gardening and increase the returns from the labor. Planting seeds and plants at random always results in waste and disappointment. Suggestions for planning a garden are here presented with the idea that they can be changed to suit the individual gardener.

The first consideration is whether the garden is to be in one unit or in two. With two plots, lettuce, radishes, beets, spinach, and other vegetables requiring little space are grown in a small kitchen garden, and potatoes, sweet corn, pumpkins, melons, and other vegetables requiring more room are planted in a separate patch, as between young-orchard-tree rows or in other areas where conditions are especially suitable for their culture.

The cultivation methods to be employed are important in planning the garden. When the work is to be done mainly with a garden tractor, the site and the arrangement should be such as to give the longest practicable rows. On slopes of more than 1½ percent, especially on light-textured soil, the rows should extend across the slope at right angles, or on the contours where the land is uneven. The garden should be free from paths across the rows, and turning spaces of 10 to 12 feet should be provided at the ends. The rows for small-growing crops may be closer together for hand cultivation than for cultivation with power equipment.

Any great variation in the composition of the soil within the garden should be taken into consideration when deciding on where to plant various crops. If part of the land is low and moist, such crops as celery, onions, and late cucumbers should be placed there. If part is high, warm, and dry, that is the proper spot for early crops, especially those needing a soil that warms up quickly.

Permanent crops, such as asparagus and rhubarb, should be planted where they will not interfere with the annual plowing of the garden and the cultivation of the annual crops. If a hotbed, a coldframe, or a special seedbed is provided, it should be either in one corner of, or outside, the garden.

Tall-growing crops should be planted where they will not shade or interfere with the growth of smaller crops. There seems to be little choice as to whether the rows do or do not run in a general east-and-west or in a general north-and-south direction, but they should conform to the contours of the land.

Succession of Crops

Except in dry-land areas, all garden space should be kept fully occupied throughout the growing season. In the South, this means the greater part of the year. In fact, throughout the South Atlantic and Gulf coast regions it is possible to have vegetables growing in the garden every month of the year.

In arranging the garden, all early-maturing crops may be grouped so that as soon as one crop is removed another takes its place. It is desirable, however, to follow a crop not with another of its kind, but with an unrelated crop. For example, early peas or beans can very properly be followed by late cabbage, celery, carrots, or beets; early corn or potatoes can be followed by fall turnips or spinach. It is not always necessary to wait until the early crop is entirely removed; a later one may be planted between the rows of the early crop—for example, sweet corn between potato rows. Crops subject to attack by the same diseases and insects should not follow each other.

In the extreme North, where the season is relatively short, there is very little opportunity for succession cropping. In dry-land areas, inter-cropping generally is not feasible, because of limited moisture supply. Therefore, plenty of land should be provided to accommodate the desired range and volume of garden crops.

Late Summer and Fall Garden

Although gardening is commonly considered mainly as a spring and early-summer enterprise, the late-summer and fall garden deserves attention too. Second and third plantings of crops adapted to growing late in the season not only provide a supply of fresh vegetables for the latter part of the season but often give better products for canning, freezing, and storing. Late-grown snap and lima beans and spinach, for example, are well adapted to freezing and canning; beets, carrots, celery, and turnips, to storage. In the South, the late-autumn garden is as important as the early-autumn one.

SELECTING SEED

Except in special cases, it pays the gardener to buy seed from reputable seedsmen and not to depend on home-grown supplies. Very fine varieties that do extremely well in certain areas have been grown for long periods from locally produced seed, and such practices are to be commended, provided adequate measures are taken to keep the strains pure.

Vegetables that are entirely, or readily, cross-pollinated *among plants of their kind* include corn, cucumbers, melons, squash, pumpkins, cress, mustard, brussels sprouts, cabbage, cauliflower, collards, kale, kohlrabi, spinach, onion, radish, beet, and turnip. Those less readily cross-pollinated are eggplant, pepper, tomato, carrot, and celery. Beans, peas, okra, and lettuce are generally self-pollinated, but occasionally cross-pollinated, lima beans sometimes rather extensively. Because sweet corn will cross with field corn, it is unwise to save sweet corn seed if field corn is growing in the same neighborhood. Hybrid sweet corn should not be saved for seed. The custom of saving seed from a choice watermelon is safe, provided no citrons or other varieties of watermelons are growing nearby. Likewise, seed from a muskmelon is safe, even though it was grown side by side with cucumbers. Beans do not readily cross and their seed also may be saved. Cabbage, kohlrabi, kale, collards, broccoli, and cauliflower all intercross freely, so each must be well isolated from the others if seed is to be saved.

Seeds should be ordered well in advance of planting time, but only after the preparation of a garden plan that shows the size of the plantings and the quantity of seed required. Table 2 shows the quantity of seed required for a given space, but allowance should be made for the possible need of replanting. Crops and varieties that are known to be adapted to the locality should be selected. The agricultural experiment station of each State, county agricultural agents, and experienced gardeners are usually able to give advice about varieties of vegetables that are adapted to the area. Standard sorts of known quality and performance are usually the best choice.

Disease-resistant strains and varieties of many important vegetables are now so generally available that there is little reason for risk-

TABLE 2.—*Quantity of seed and number of plants required for 100 feet of row, depths of planting, and distances apart for rows and plants*

Crop	Requirement for 100 feet of row		Depth for planting seed	Distance apart		
	Seed	Plants		Rows		Plants in the row
				Horse- or tractor-cultivated	Hand-cultivated	
			Inches	*Feet*		
Asparagus	1 ounce	75	1 –1½	4 –5	1½ to 2 feet	18 inches.
Beans:						
Lima, bush	½ pound		1 –1½	2½–3	2 feet	3 to 4 inches.
Lima, pole	½ pound		1 –1½	3 –4	3 feet	3 to 4 feet.
Snap, bush	½ pound		1 –1½	2½–3	2 feet	3 to 4 inches.
Snap, pole	4 ounces		1 –1½	3 –4	2 feet	3 feet.
Beet	2 ounces		1	2 –2½	14 to 16 inches	2 to 3 inches.
Broccoli:						
Heading	1 packet	50– 75	½	2½–3	2 to 2½ feet	14 to 24 inches.
Sprouting	1 packet	50– 75	½	2½–3	2 to 2½ feet	14 to 24 inches.
Brussels sprouts	1 packet	50– 75	½	2½–3	2 to 2½ feet	14 to 24 inches.
Cabbage	1 packet	50– 75	½	2½–3	2 to 2½ feet	14 to 24 inches.
Cabbage, Chinese	1 packet		½	2 –2½	18 to 24 inches	8 to 12 inches.
Carrot	1 packet		½	2 –2½	14 to 16 inches	2 to 3 inches.
Cauliflower	1 packet	50– 75	½	2½–3	2 to 2½ feet	14 to 24 inches.
Celeriac	1 packet	200–250	⅛	2½–3	18 to 24 inches	4 to 6 inches.
Celery	1 packet	200–250	⅛	2½–3	18 to 24 inches	4 to 6 inches.
Chard	2 ounces		1	2 –2½	18 to 24 inches	6 inches.
Chervil	1 packet		½	2 –2½	14 to 16 inches	2 to 3 inches.

Chicory, witloof	1 packet		½	2 –2½	18 to 24 inches	6 to 8 inches.
Chives	1 packet		½	2½–3	14 to 16 inches	In clusters.
Collards	1 packet		½	3 –3½	18 to 24 inches	18 to 24 inches.
Cornsalad	1 packet		½	2½–3	14 to 16 inches	1 foot.
Corn, sweet	2 ounces		2	3 –3½	2 to 3 feet	Drills, 14 to 16 inches; hills, 2½ to 3 feet.
Cress Upland	1 packet		⅛– ¼	2 –2½	14 to 16 inches	2 to 3 inches.
Cucumber	1 packet		½	6 –7	6 to 7 feet	Drills, 3 feet; hills, 6 feet.
Dasheen	5 to 6 pounds	50	2 –3	3½–4	3½ to 4 feet	2 feet.
Eggplant	1 packet	50	½	3	2 to 2½ feet	3 feet.
Endive	1 packet		½	2½–3	18 to 24 inches	12 inches.
Fennel, Florence	1 packet		½	2½–3	18 to 24 inches	4 to 6 inches.
Garlic	1 pound		1 –2	2½–3	14 to 16 inches	2 to 3 inches.
Horseradish	Cuttings	50–75	2	3 –4	2 to 2½ feet	18 to 24 inches.
Kale	1 packet		½	2½–3	18 to 24 inches	12 to 15 inches.
Kohlrabi	1 packet		½	2½–3	14 to 16 inches	5 to 6 inches.
Leek	1 packet		½–1	2½–3	14 to 16 inches	2 to 3 inches.
Lettuce, head	1 packet	100	½	2½–3	14 to 16 inches	12 to 15 inches.
Lettuce, leaf	1 packet		½	2½–3	14 to 16 inches	6 inches.
Muskmelon	1 packet		1	6 –7	6 to 7 feet	Hills, 6 feet.
Mustard	1 packet		½	2½–3	14 to 16 inches	12 inches.
Okra	2 ounces		1 –1½	3 –3½	3 to 3½ feet	2 feet.
Onion:						
Plants		400	1 –2	2 –2½	14 to 16 inches	2 to 3 inches.
Seed	1 packet		½–1	2 –2½	14 to 16 inches	2 to 3 inches.
Sets	1 pound		1 –2	2 –2½	14 to 16 inches	2 to 3 inches.
Parsley	1 packet		⅛	2 –2½	14 to 16 inches	4 to 6 inches.
Parsley, turnip-rooted	1 packet		⅛– ¼	2 –2½	14 to 16 inches	2 to 3 inches.
Parsnip	1 packet		½	2 –2½	18 to 24 inches	2 to 3 inches.
Peas	½ pound		2 –3	2 –4	1½ to 3 feet	1 inch.
Pepper	1 packet	50–70	½	3 –4	2 to 3 feet	18 to 24 inches.
Physalis	1 packet		½	2 –2½	1½ to 2 feet	12 to 18 inches.

TABLE 2.—Quantity of seed and number of plants required for 100 feet of row, depths of planting, and distances apart for rows and plants—continued

| Crop | Requirement for 100 feet of row | | Depth for planting seed | Distance apart | | |
| | Seed | Plants | | Rows | | Plants in the row |
				Horse- or tractor-cultivated	Hand-cultivated	
Potato	5 to 6 pounds, tubers		4	2½–3	2 to 2½ feet	10 to 18 inches.
Pumpkin	1 ounce		1 –2	5 –8	5 to 8 feet	3 to 4 feet.
Radish	1 ounce		½	2 –2½	14 to 16 inches	1 inch.
Rhubarb		25–35	----	3 –4	3 to 4 feet	3 to 4 feet.
Salsify	1 ounce		½	2 –2½	18 to 26 inches	2 to 3 inches.
Shallots	1 pound (cloves)		1 –2	2 –2½	12 to 18 inches	2 to 3 inches.
Sorrel	1 packet		½	2 –2½	18 to 24 inches	5 to 8 inches.
Soybean	½ to 1 pound		1 –1½	2½–3	24 to 30 inches	3 inches.
Spinach	1 ounce		½	2 –2½	14 to 16 inches	3 to 4 inches.
Spinach, New Zealand	1 ounce		1 –1½	3 –3½	3 feet	18 inches.
Squash:						
Bush	½ ounce		1 –2	4 –5	4 to 5 feet	Drills, 15 to 18 inches; hills, 4 feet.
Vine	1 ounce		1 –2	8 –12	8 to 12 feet	Drills, 2 to 3 feet; hills, 4 feet.
Sweetpotato	5 pounds, bedroots	75	2 –3	3 –3½	3 to 3½ feet	12 to 14 inches.
Tomato	1 packet	35–50	½	3 –4	2 to 3 feet	1½ to 3 feet.
Turnip greens	1 packet		¼–½	2 –2½	14 to 16 inches	2 to 3 inches.
Turnips and rutabagas	½ ounce		¼–½	2 –2½	14 to 16 inches	2 to 3 inches.
Watermelon	1 ounce		1 –2	8 –10	8 to 10 feet	Drills, 2 to 3 feet; hills, 8 feet.

ing the loss of a crop through planting susceptible sorts. This phase of the subject is
treated in detail under the individual crops.
Some seeds retain their vitality longer than
others. Seeds may be divided into three groups
as follows: (1) Comparatively short-lived, usually not good after 1 to 2 years—corn, leek,
onion, parsley, parsnip, rhubarb and salsify;
(2) moderately long-lived, often good for 3 to
5 years—asparagus, beans, brussels sprouts,
cabbage, carrot, cauliflower, celery, kale, lettuce, okra, peas, pepper, radish, spinach, turnip and watermelon; and (3) long-lived, may
be good for more than 5 years—beet, cucumber,
eggplant, muskmelon, and tomato.

STARTING THE PLANTS

Table 2 gives in general the proper depth of
planting for seed of the various vegetables, the
quantity of seed or number of plants required
for 100 feet of row, and the correct spacing of
rows and of plants within the row. Special
planting suggestions are given in the cultural
hints for the various garden crops.

Earliness, economy of garden space, and
lengthening of the growing season may be obtained by setting the plants of many vegetables
instead of sowing the seed directly in the garden. Moreover, it is almost impossible to estab-
lish good stands from seed sown directly in
place in the garden with delicate plants, such
as celery, under average conditions.

In the warmer parts of the United States,

practically all vegetable plants may be started in specially prepared beds in the open with little or no covering. In the temperate and colder regions, if an early garden is desired, it is essential that certain crops, such as tomatoes, peppers, eggplant, early cabbage, cauliflower, and early head lettuce, be started indoors, in hotbeds, or in coldframes. Occasionally onion, beet, cucumber, squash, and melons are started under cover and transplanted.

Starting Plants in the House

Seeds can be germinated and seedlings started in a box, pan, or flowerpot of soil in a window. In addition to having at least 6 hours of direct sunlight each day, the room must be kept reasonably warm at all times.

Washed fine sand and shredded sphagnum moss are excellent media in which to start seeds. Place a layer of easily drained soil in the bottom of a flat and cover this soil with a layer —about three-fourths inch thick—of either fine sand or sphagnum moss. Press the sand or moss to form a smooth, firm seedbed.

Then, using a jig (fig. 4), make furrows in the seedbed one-half inch deep. Water the sand or moss thoroughly and allow it to drain.

Sow seeds thinly in the rows and cover the seeds lightly with a second layer of sand or moss. Sprinkle the flat, preferably with a fine mist, and cover the flat with a sheet of clear plastic film (fig. 5). The plastic film diffuses and subdues the light and holds moisture in the soil and air surrounding the seeds. Plastic films offer advantages over glass coverings in that they are light in weight and are nonshattering.

PN-2613
Figure 4.—One-half-inch furrows made with a jig.

PN-2614
Figure 5.—Clear plastic film gives a flat, even,
subdued light and holds the moisture.

Place the seeded and covered flat in a location that is reasonably warm at all times and has 6 hours of direct sunlight each day. The flat will require no further attention until after the seedlings have developed their first true leaves (fig. 6). They are then ready to transplant to other containers.

It is seldom possible to keep the transplanted plants in house windows without their becoming spindling and weak. For healthy growth,

PN–2615

Figure 6.—Seedlings with first true leaves ready for transplanting.

place them in a hotbed, coldframe, or other place where they will receive an abundance of sunshine, ample ventilation, and a suitable temperature.

Strong, vigorous seedlings can be started

under 40-watt fluorescent tubes (fig. 7). These tubes should be 6 to 8 inches above the seedlings. Temperatures should be about 60° F. at night and 70° during the day. Best results are obtained if the fluorescent fixture is next to a window to increase the amount of light reaching the young plants.

Soil pellets are the simplest and easiest method for starting plants and are readily

PN–2616
Figure 7.—Starting plants under fluorescent light opposite a window.

available from garden supply stores and other sources. Soil pellets are a well-balanced synthetic soil mixture and are free of soilborne diseases and weeds (fig. 8).

Special Devices for Starting Plants

In determining the type of equipment for starting early plants, the gardener must consider the temperature and other climatic con-

PN–2617

Figure 8.—Soil pellets, left to right, unmoistened, moistened with emerging seedling, and lettuce plant ready to plant in the garden.

PN–2618

Figure 9.—Growing early plants in a glass coldframe located on the south side of the house. Some heat is applied from the basement window.

ditions in his locality, as well as the nature of the plants to be started. Hardy plants, such as cabbage, need only simple inexpensive facilities, but such heat-loving, tender seedlings as peppers and eggplant must have more elaborate facilities for successful production. In the warmer parts of the United States, and in the well-protected locations elsewhere, a coldframe or a sash-covered pit on the sunny side of a building usually suffices (fig. 9). In colder sections, or in exposed areas elsewhere, some form of artificial heat is essential. Where only a little protection against cold damage, at infrequent intervals, is needed, a coldframe in which a temporary bank of lamps can be placed may be sufficient. The hotbed, lean-to, or sash greenhouse heated by manure, pipes, flues, or electricity are all widely used, the choice depending on conditions. A comparatively small plant-growing structure will provide enough plants for several gardens, and joint efforts by a number of gardeners will usually reduce the labor of producing plants.

The plant-growing structure should always be on well-drained land free from danger of flooding. A sunny, southern exposure on a moderate slope, with trees, a hedge, a board fence, or other form of windbreak on the north and west, makes a desirable site. Plenty of sunshine is necessary.

Hotbeds and other plant-growing devices require close attention. They must be ventilated at frequent intervals, and the plants may require watering more than once daily. Convenience in handling the work is important. Sudden storms may necessitate closing the structure within a matter of minutes. Plant growing at home should not be undertaken by persons obliged to be away for extended periods, leaving the plant structure unattended.

A tight well-glazed structure is necessary where the climate is severe; less expensive facilities are satisfactory elsewhere.

Covers for hotbeds and coldframes may be glass sash, fiber glass, plastic film, muslin, or light canvas.

In the moderate and cooler sections of the country, standard 3- by 6-foot hotbed sash is most satisfactory. Even this requires supplementary covering with canvas, blankets, mats, or similar material during freezing weather. The amount of covering is determined by the degree of heat supplied the structure, the severity of the weather, and the kind of plants and their stage of development. Farther South, where less protection is necessary, a muslin cover may be all that is needed and for only a part of the time.

Many substitutes for glass as coverings for hotbeds and coldframes are on the market. The most widely used substitutes are various kinds of clear plastic film. Some of these have a lifespan of only one season, and others a lifespan of 3 to 5 years.

Clear plastic film transmits as much light as glass in the visible range, and more than glass in the ultraviolet and infrared ranges.

The film comes as flat sheets (on rolls) and in tubular form. Flat-sheet film is used for tacking onto wooden frames; the tubular form is used for enclosing metal tubular frames with a tight double layer of film.

Figure 10. A double layer of plastic film supported by semicircular galvanized pipe makes a highly satisfactory portable coldframe.

Large plant hoods made from semicircular aluminum or galvanized steel pipe and fitted with a sleeve of tubular plastic film (fig. 10) make excellent coldframes or seasonal row covers. When used in this way, a double layer of plastic film provides an air space that insulates against 4° to 7° of frost temperature change.

Electrically heated plant beds are ideal for the home gardener, provided electric rates are not too high. The beds may be built any size. Because they are equipped with thermostatic control, they require a minimum of attention. It is now possible to buy frames—completely equipped with heating cables, switches, and thermostats—ready to assemble and set in position. Fill the frames with soil or plant boxes and connect to a source of current (fig. 11). Small frames may be removed at the end of the season and stored; larger frames are usually treated as a permanent installation. For more detailed information, see USDA Leaflet 445, Electric Heating of Hotbeds.

Hardening Plants

Plants should be gradually hardened, or toughened, for 2 weeks before planting in the open garden. This is done by slowing down their rate of growth to prepare them to withstand such conditions as chilling, drying winds, shortage of water, or high temperatures. Cabbage, lettuce, onion, and many other plants can be hardened to withstand frost; others, such as tomatoes and peppers cannot. Withholding water and lowering the temperature are the best ways to harden a plant. This may be done in a glass or plastic coldframe.

About 10 days before being planted in the open ground, the young plants in beds or flats

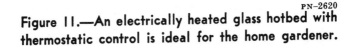

ELECTRICAL OUTLET

THERMOSTAT

GLASS SASH (OR PLASTIC COVER)

WEATHERSTRIP

REMOTE BULB

HEATING CABLE

1" to 2" SAND OR SOIL

HARDWARE CLOTH

4" to 5" SOIL

PN-2620

Figure 11.—An electrically heated glass hotbed with thermostatic control is ideal for the home gardener.

are blocked out with a large knife. Blocking, or cutting the roots, causes new roots to form quickly near the plants, making recovery from transplanting in the open easier. Blocking also makes it easier to remove the plants from the bed or flat with minimum injury.

Southern-Grown Plants

Vegetable plants grown outdoors in the South are shipped to all parts of the country. They are grown cheaply and usually withstand shipment and resetting very well. They may not always be as good as home-grown plants, but they save the trouble of starting them in the house or in a hot-bed. Plants of beets, brussels sprouts, cabbage, cauliflower, lettuce, onions, peppers, and tomatoes are extensively grown and shipped; tomato, cabbage, and onion plants make up the bulk of the shipments. The plants are usually wrapped in bundles of 50 each and shipped by either mail or express. Tomato and pepper plants are packed with a little damp moss around the roots, but onion and cabbage plants are usually packed with bare roots. Shipments involving large numbers of bundles are packed in ventilated hampers or slatted crates and usually are sent by motor-truck or rail express. Shipments by air mail and air express are increasing.

The disadvantages of using southern-grown plants are the occasional delays in obtaining them and the possibility of transmitting such diseases as the wilt disease of the tomato, black rot of cabbage, and disorders caused by nematodes. State-certified plants that have been carefully inspected and found as free of these troubles as can be reasonably determined are available. Southern-grown plants are now offered for sale by most northern seedsmen, by mail-order houses, and often by local hardware and supply houses.

Transplanting

The term "transplanting" means shifting of a plant from one soil or culture medium to another. It may refer to the shifting of small seedlings from the seedbed to other containers where the plants will have more space for growth, or it may mean the setting of plants in the garden row where they are to develop for the crop period. Contrary to general belief, transplanting does not in itself stimulate the plant or make it grow better; actually growth is temporarily checked, but the plant is usually given more space in which to grow. Every effort should be made during transplanting to interrupt the growth of the plant as little as possible.

Plants started in seed flats, flowerpots, and other containers in the house, the hotbed, the greenhouse, or elsewhere should be shifted as soon as they can be handled to boxes, flowerpots, plant bands, or other containers where they will have more room to develop. If shifted to flats or similar containers, the plants should be spaced 2 or more inches apart. This provides room for growth until the plants can be moved to their permanent place in the garden. Most gardeners prefer to place seedlings singly in flowerpots, paper cups with the bottoms pierced for drainage, plant bands, berry boxes, or other containers. When the plants are set in the garden, the containers are carefully removed.

Soil for transplanting should be fertile, usually a mixture of rich topsoil and garden compost, with a very light addition of a commercial garden fertilizer.

Moistening the seedbed before removing the seedlings and care in lifting and separating the delicate plants make it possible to shift them with little damage to the root system and with only minor checks to their growth. Plants grown singly in separate containers can be moved to the garden with almost no disturbance to the root system, especially those that are hardened for a week or two before being set outdoors. Plants being hardened should be watered sparingly, but just before they are set out, they should be given a thorough soaking.

Plants grown in the hotbed or greenhouse

without being shifted from the seedbed to provide more room and those shipped from the South usually have very little soil adhering to the roots when they are set in the garden. Such plants may require special care if transplanting conditions are not ideal; otherwise, they will die or at least suffer a severe shock that will greatly retard their development. The roots of these plants should be kept covered and not allowed to dry out. Dipping the roots in a mixture of clay and water helps greatly in bridging the critical transplanting period. Planting when the soil is moist also helps. Pouring a half pint to a pint of water, or less for small plants, into the hole around the plant before it is completely filled is usually necessary. A starter solution made by mixing ½ pound of a 4–12–4 or 5–10–5 commercial fertilizer in 4 gallons of water may be used instead of plain water. It is usually beneficial. Finally, the freshly set plants should be shaded for a day or two with newspapers.

Plants differ greatly in the way they recover from the loss of roots and from exposure to new conditions. Small plants of tomatoes, lettuce, beets, cabbage, and related vegetables are easy to transplant. They withstand the treatment better than peppers, eggplant, and the vine crops. When started indoors and moved to the field, the vine crops should be seeded directly in berry baskets or containers of the same size that can be transferred to the garden and removed without disturbing the root systems. Beans and sweet corn can be handled in the same manner, thereby often gaining a week or two in earliness.

PLANTING THE GARDEN

One of the most important elements of success in growing vegetables is planting, or transplanting, each crop at the time or times that are best for the operation in each locality. Temperatures often differ so much between localities not many miles apart that the best planting dates for some one vegetable may differ by several days or even 2 weeks.

Vegetable crops may be roughly grouped and sown according to their hardiness and their temperature requirements. A rough timetable for planting some of the commoner crops is shown in table 3, based on the frost-free dates in spring and fall. The frost-free date in spring is usually 2 to 3 weeks later than the average date of the last freeze in a locality and is approximately the date that oak trees leaf out.

The gardener naturally wants to make the first planting of each vegetable as early as he can without too much danger of its being damaged by cold. Many vegetables are so hardy to cold that they can be planted a month or more before the average date of the last freeze, or about 6 weeks before the frost-free date. Furthermore, most, if not all, cold-tolerant crops actually thrive better in cool weather than in hot weather and should not be planted late in the spring in the southern two-thirds of the country where summers are hot. Thus, **the** gardener must time his planting not only **to** escape cold but with certain crops also to escape heat. Some vegetables that will not thrive when planted in late spring in areas having rather hot summers may be sown in late summer, however, so that they will make most of their growth in cooler weather.

TABLE 3.—*Some common vegetables grouped according to the approximate times they can be planted and their relative requirements for cool and warm weather*

Cold-hardy plants for early-spring planting		Cold-tender or heat-hardy plants for later-spring or early-summer planting			Hardy plants for late-summer or fall planting except in the North (plant 6 to 8 weeks before first fall freeze)
Very hardy (plant 4 to 6 weeks before frost-free date)	Hardy (plant 2 to 4 weeks before frost-free date)	Not cold-hardy (plant on frost-free date)	Requiring hot weather (plant 1 week or more after frost-free date)	Medium heat-tolerant (good for summer planting)	
Broccoli	Beets	Beans,	Beans,	Beans, all	Beets
Cabbage	Carrot	snap	lima	Chard	Collard
Lettuce	Chard	Okra	Eggplant	Soybean	Kale
Onions	Mustard	New Zea-	Peppers	New Zea-	Lettuce
Peas	Parsnip	land	Sweetpo-	land	Mustard
Potato	Radish	spinach	tato	spinach	Spinach
Spinach		Soybean	Cucum-	Squash	Turnip
Turnip		Squash	ber	Sweet	
		Sweet corn	Melons	corn	
		Tomato			

A gardener anywhere in the United States can determine his own safe planting dates for different crops by using the maps (figs. 12 and 13), together with tables 4 and 5, in this bulletin. The maps show the average dates of the last killing frosts in spring and the average dates of the first killing frosts in fall. They are the dates from which planting times can be determined, and such determinations have been so worked out in tables 4 and 5 that any gardener can use them, with only a little trouble, to find out the planting dates for his locality.

Table 4, for use with the map in figure 12, shows planting dates between January 1 and June 30, covering chiefly spring and early-summer crops. It shows *how early it is safe to plant;* it also shows the spring and early-summer dates *beyond which planting usually gives poor results.*

Opposite each vegetable in table 4, the first date in any column is the *earliest generally safe* date that the crop can be sown or transplanted by the gardener using that column. (No gardener needs to use more than one of the columns.) The second date is the latest date that is likely to prove satisfactory for the planting. All times in between these two dates may not, however, give equally good results. Most of the crops listed do better when planted not too far from the earlier date shown.

To determine the best time to plant any vegetable in the spring in your locality:

1. Find your location on the map in figure 12 and then, the solid line on the map that comes nearest to it.

2. Find the date shown on the solid line. This is the average date of the last killing frost. The first number represents the month; the second number, the day. Thus, 3–10 is March 10. Once you know the date you are through with the map.

3. Turn to table 4; find the column that has your date over it; and draw a heavy line around this entire column. It is the only date column in the table that you will need.

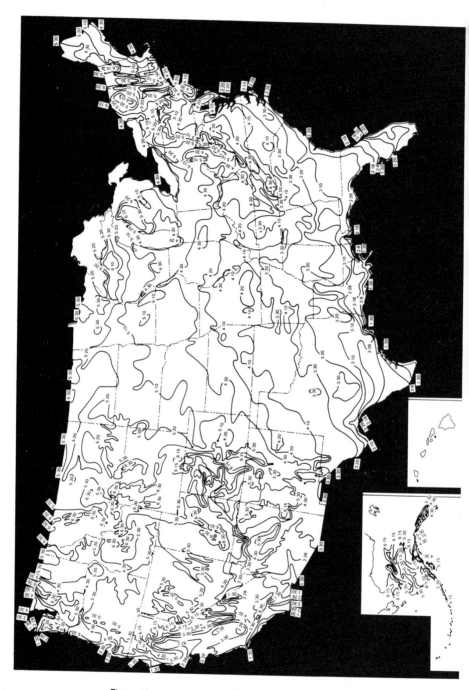

Figure 12.—Average dates of the last killing frost in spring.

4. Find the dates in the column that are on a line with the name of the crop you want to plant. These dates show the period during which the crop can safely be planted. The best time is on, or soon after, the first of the two dates. A time halfway between them is very good; the second date is not so good.

For areas in the Plains region that warm up quickly in the spring and are subject to dry weather, very early planting is essential to escape heat and drought. In fact, most of the cool-season crops do not thrive when spring-planted in the southern part of the Great Plains and southern Texas.

Table 5 is used with the map in figure 13 in the same way to find the dates for late plantings. The recommendations for late plantings and for those in the South for overwintered crops are less exact and less dependable than those for early planting. Factors other than direct temperature effects—summer rainfall, for example, and the severity of diseases and insects—often make success difficult, especially in the Southeast, although some other areas having the same frost dates are more favorable. A date about halfway between the two shown in table 5 will generally be best, although in most areas fair success can be expected within the entire range of dates shown.

Along the northern half of the Pacific coast, warm-weather crops should not be planted quite so late as the frost date and table would indicate. Although frost comes late, very cool weather prevails for some time before frost, retarding late growth of crops like sweet corn, lima beans, and tomatoes.

TABLE 4.—*Earliest dates, and range of dates, for safe*

Crop	Planting dates for localities		
	Jan. 30	Feb. 8	Feb. 18
Asparagus [1]			
Beans, lima	Feb. 1–Apr. 15	Feb. 10–May 1	Mar. 1–May 1
Beans, snap	Feb. 1–Apr. 1	Feb. 1–May 1	Mar. 1–May 1
Beet	Jan. 1–Mar. 15	Jan. 10–Mar. 15	Jan. 20–Apr. 1
Broccoli, sprouting [1]	Jan. 1–30	Jan. 1–30	Jan. 15–Feb. 15
Brussels sprouts [1]	Jan. 1–30	Jan. 1–30	Jan. 15–Feb. 15
Cabbage [1]	Jan. 1–15	Jan. 1–Feb. 10	Jan. 1–Feb. 25
Cabbage, Chinese	(²)	(²)	(²)
Carrot	Jan. 1–Mar. 1	Jan. 1–Mar. 1	Jan. 15–Mar. 1
Cauliflower [1]	Jan. 1–Feb. 1	Jan. 1–Feb. 1	Jan. 10–Feb. 10
Celery and celeriac	Jan. 1–Feb. 1	Jan. 10–Feb. 10	Jan. 20–Feb. 20
Chard	Jan. 1–Apr. 1	Jan. 10–Apr. 1	Jan. 20–Apr. 15
Chervil and chives	Jan. 1–Feb. 1	Jan. 1–Feb. 1	Jan. 1–Feb. 1
Chicory, witloof			
Collards [1]	Jan. 1–Feb. 15	Jan. 1–Feb. 15	Jan. 1–Mar. 15
Cornsalad	Jan. 1–Feb. 15	Jan. 1–Feb. 15	Jan. 1–Mar. 15
Corn, sweet	Feb. 1–Mar. 15	Feb. 10–Apr. 1	Feb. 20–Apr. 15
Cress, upland	Jan. 1–Feb. 1	Jan. 1–Feb. 15	Jan. 15–Feb. 15
Cucumber	Feb. 15–Mar. 15	Feb. 15–Apr. 1	Feb. 15–Apr. 15
Eggplant [1]	Feb. 1–Mar. 1	Feb. 10–Mar. 15	Feb. 20–Apr. 1
Endive	Jan. 1–Mar. 1	Jan. 1–Mar. 1	Jan. 15–Mar. 1
Fennel, Florence	Jan. 1–Mar. 1	Jan. 1–Mar. 1	Jan. 15–Mar. 1
Garlic	(²)	(²)	(²)
Horseradish [1]			
Kale	Jan. 1–Feb. 1	Jan. 10–Feb. 1	Jan. 20–Feb. 10
Kohlrabi	Jan. 1–Feb. 1	Jan. 10–Feb. 1	Jan. 20–Feb. 10
Leek	Jan. 1–Feb. 1	Jan. 1–Feb. 1	Jan. 1–Feb. 15
Lettuce, head [1]	Jan. 1–Feb. 1	Jan. 1–Feb. 1	Jan. 1–Feb. 1
Lettuce, leaf	Jan. 1–Feb. 1	Jan. 1–Feb. 1	Jan. 1–Mar. 15
Muskmelon	Feb. 15–Mar. 15	Feb. 15–Apr. 1	Feb. 15–Apr. 15
Mustard	Jan. 1–Mar. 1	Jan. 1–Mar. 1	Feb. 15–Apr. 15
Okra	Feb. 15–Apr. 1	Feb. 15–Apr. 15	Mar. 1–June 1
Onion [1]	Jan. 1–15	Jan. 1–15	Jan. 1–15
Onion, seed	Jan. 1–15	Jan. 1–15	Jan. 1–15
Onion, sets	Jan. 1–15	Jan. 1–15	Jan. 1–15
Parsley	Jan. 1–30	Jan. 1–30	Jan. 1–30
Parsnip			
Peas, garden	Jan. 1–Feb. 15	Jan. 1–Feb. 15	Jan. 1–Feb. 1
Peas, black-eye	Feb. 15–May 1	Feb. 15–May 15	Jan. 1–Mar. 1
Pepper [1]	Feb. 1–Apr. 1	Feb. 15–Apr. 15	Mar. 1–June 15
Potato	Jan. 1–Feb. 15	Feb. 15–Apr. 15	Mar. 1–May 1
Radish	Jan. 1–Apr. 1	Jan. 1–Feb. 15	Jan. 15–Mar. 1
Rhubarb [1]		Jan. 1–Apr. 1	Jan. 1–Apr. 1
Rutabaga			
Salsify	Jan. 1–Feb. 1	Jan. 10–Feb. 10	Jan. 15–Feb. 20
Shallot	Jan. 1–Feb. 1	Jan. 1–Feb. 10	Jan. 1–Feb. 20
Sorrel	Jan. 1–Mar. 1	Jan. 1–Mar. 1	Jan. 15–Mar. 1
Soybean	Mar. 1–June 30	Mar. 1–June 30	Mar. 10–June 30
Spinach	Jan. 1–Feb. 15	Jan. 1–Feb. 15	Jan. 1–Mar. 1
Spinach, New Zealand	Feb. 1–Apr. 15	Feb. 15–Apr. 15	Mar. 1–Apr. 15
Squash, summer	Feb. 1–Apr. 15	Feb. 15–Apr. 15	Mar. 1–Apr. 15
Sweetpotato	Feb. 15–May 15	Mar. 1–May 15	Mar. 20–June 1
Tomato	Feb. 1–Apr. 1	Feb. 20–Apr. 10	Mar. 1–Apr. 20
Turnip	Jan. 1–Mar. 1	Jan. 1–Mar. 1	Jan. 10–Mar. 1
Watermelon	Feb. 15–Mar. 15	Feb. 15–Apr. 1	Feb. 15–Apr. 15

[1] Plants.
[²] Generally fall-planted (table 5).

spring planting of vegetables in the open

in which average date of last freeze is—

Feb. 28	Mar. 10	Mar. 20	Mar. 30
	Jan. 1–Mar. 1	Feb. 1–Mar. 10	Feb. 15–Mar. 20.
Mar. 15–June 1	Mar. 20–June 1	Apr. 1–June 15	Apr. 15–June 20.
Mar. 10–May 15	Mar. 15–May 15	Mar. 15–May 25	Apr. 1–June 1.
Feb. 1–Apr. 15	Feb. 15–June 1	Feb. 15–May 15	Mar. 1–June 1.
Feb. 1–Mar. 1	Feb. 15–Mar. 15	Feb. 15–Mar. 15	Mar. 1–20.
Feb. 1–Mar. 1	Feb. 15–Mar. 15	Feb. 15–Mar. 15	Mar. 1–20.
Jan. 15–Feb. 25	Jan. 25–Mar. 1	Feb. 1–Mar. 1	Feb. 15–Mar. 10.
(2)	(2)	(2)	(2)
Feb. 1–Mar. 1	Feb. 10–Mar. 15	Feb. 15–Mar. 20	Mar. 1–Apr. 10.
Jan. 20–Feb. 20	Feb. 1–Mar. 1	Feb. 10–Mar. 10	Feb. 20–Mar. 20.
Feb. 1–Mar. 1	Feb. 20–Mar. 20	Mar. 1–Apr. 1	Mar. 15–Apr. 15.
Feb. 1–May 1	Feb. 15–May 15	Feb. 20–May 15	Mar. 1–May 25.
Jan. 15–Feb. 15	Feb. 1–Mar. 1	Feb. 10–Mar. 10	Feb. 15–Mar. 15.
	June 1–July 1	June 1–July 1	June 1–July 1.
Jan. 15–Mar. 15	Feb. 1–Apr. 1	Feb. 15–May 1	Mar. 1–June 1.
Jan. 1–Mar. 1	Jan. 1–Mar. 15	Jan. 1–Mar. 15	Jan. 15–Mar. 15.
Mar. 1–Apr. 15	Mar. 10–Apr. 15	Mar. 15–May 1	Mar. 25–May 15.
Feb. 1–Mar. 1	Feb. 10–Mar. 15	Feb. 20–Mar. 15	Mar. 1–Apr. 1.
Mar. 1–Apr. 15	Mar. 15–Apr. 15	Apr. 1–May 1	Apr. 10–May 15.
Mar. 10–Apr. 15	Mar. 15–Apr. 15	Apr. 1–May 1	Apr. 15–May 15.
Feb. 1–Mar. 1	Feb. 15–Mar. 15	Mar. 1–Apr. 1	Mar. 10–Apr. 10.
Feb. 1–Mar. 1	Feb. 15–Mar. 15	Mar. 1–Apr. 1	Mar. 10–Apr. 10.
(2)	(2)	Feb. 1–Mar. 1	Feb. 10–Mar. 10.
			Mar. 1–Apr. 1.
Feb. 1–20	Feb. 10–Mar. 1	Feb. 20–Mar. 10	Mar. 1–20.
Feb. 1–20	Feb. 10–Mar. 1	Feb. 20–Mar. 10	Mar. 1–Apr. 1.
Jan. 15–Feb. 15	Jan. 25–Mar. 1	Feb. 1–Mar. 1	Feb. 15–Mar. 15.
Jan. 15–Feb. 15	Feb. 1–20	Feb. 15–Mar. 10	Mar. 1–20.
Jan. 1–Mar. 15	Jan. 15–Apr. 1	Feb. 1–Apr. 1	Feb. 15–Apr. 15.
Mar. 1–Apr. 15	Mar. 15–Apr. 15	Apr. 1–May 1	Apr. 10–May 15.
Feb. 1–Mar. 1	Feb. 10–Mar. 15	Feb. 20–Apr. 1	Mar. 1–Apr. 1.
Mar. 10–June 1	Mar. 20–June 1	Apr. 1–June 15	Apr. 10–June 15.
Jan. 1–Feb. 1	Jan. 15–Feb. 15	Feb. 10–Mar. 10	Feb. 15–Mar. 15.
Jan. 1–Feb. 15	Feb. 1–Mar. 1	Feb. 10–Mar. 10	Feb. 20–Mar. 15.
Jan. 1–Mar. 1	Jan. 15–Mar. 10	Feb. 1–Mar. 20	Feb. 15–Mar. 20.
Jan. 15–Mar. 1	Feb. 1–Mar. 10	Feb. 15–Mar. 15	Mar. 1–Apr. 1.
Jan. 15–Feb. 15	Jan. 15–Mar. 1	Feb. 15–Mar. 15	Mar. 1–Apr. 1.
Jan. 15–Mar. 1	Jan. 15–Mar. 15	Feb. 1–Mar. 15	Feb. 10–Mar. 20.
Mar. 10–June 20	Mar. 15–July 1	Apr. 1–July 1	Apr. 15–July 1.
Mar. 15–May 1	Apr. 1–June 1	Apr. 10–June 1	Apr. 15–June 1.
Jan. 15–Mar. 1	Feb. 1–Mar. 1	Feb. 10–Mar. 15	Feb. 20–Mar. 20.
Jan. 1–Apr. 1	Jan. 1–Apr. 15	Jan. 20–May 1	Feb. 15–May 1.
Jan. 1–Feb. 1	Jan. 15–Feb. 15	Jan. 15–Mar. 1	Feb. 1–Mar. 1.
Jan. 15–Mar. 1	Feb. 1–Mar. 1	Feb. 15–May 15	Mar. 1–15.
Jan. 1–Mar. 1	Jan. 15–Mar. 1	Feb. 1–Mar. 10	Feb. 15–Mar. 15.
Feb. 1–Mar. 10	Feb. 10–Mar. 15	Feb. 10–Mar. 20	Feb. 20–Apr. 1.
Mar. 20–June 30	Apr. 10–June 30	Apr. 10–June 30	Apr. 20–June 30.
Jan. 1–Mar. 1	Jan. 15–Mar. 10	Jan. 15–Mar. 15	Feb. 1–Mar. 20.
Mar. 15–May 15	Mar. 20–May 15	Apr. 1–May 15	Apr. 10–June 1.
Mar. 15–May 15	Apr. 1–June 1	Apr. 1–May 15	Apr. 10–June 1.
Mar. 20–June 1	Mar. 20–May 10	Apr. 10–June 1	Apr. 20–June 1.
Mar. 10–May 1	Feb. 1–Mar. 1	Apr. 1–May 20	Apr. 10–June 1.
Jan. 20–Mar. 1	Mar. 15–Apr. 15	Feb. 10–Mar. 10	Feb. 20–Mar. 20.
Mar. 1–Apr. 15		Apr. 1–May 1	Apr. 10–May 15.

TABLE 4.—*Earliest dates, and range of dates, for safe*

Crop	Planting dates for localities		
	Apr. 10	Apr. 20	Apr. 30
Asparagus [1]	Mar. 10–Apr. 10	Mar. 15–Apr. 15	Mar. 20–Apr. 15
Beans, lima	Apr. 1–June 30	May 1–June 20	May 15–June 15
Beans, snap	Apr. 10–June 30	Apr. 25–June 30	May 10–June 30
Beet	Mar. 10–June 1	Mar. 20–June 1	Apr. 1–June 15
Broccoli, sprouting [1]	Mar. 15–Apr. 15	Mar. 25–Apr. 20	Apr. 1–May 1
Brussels sprouts [1]	Mar. 15–Apr. 15	Mar. 25–Apr. 20	Apr. 1–May 1
Cabbage [1]	Mar. 1–Apr. 1	Mar. 10–Apr. 1	Mar. 15–Apr. 10
Cabbage, Chinese	([2])	([2])	([2])
Carrot	Mar. 10–Apr. 20	Apr. 1–May 15	Apr. 10–June 1
Cauliflower [1]	Mar. 1–Mar. 20	Mar. 15–Apr. 20	Apr. 10–May 10
Celery and celeriac	Apr. 1–Apr. 20	Apr. 10–May 1	Apr. 15–May 1
Chard	Mar. 15–June 15	Apr. 1–June 15	Apr. 15–June 15
Chervil and chives	Mar. 1–Apr. 1	Mar. 10–Apr. 10	Mar. 20–Apr. 20
Chicory, witloof	June 10–July 1	June 15–July 1	June 15–July 1
Collards [1]	Mar. 1–June 1	Mar. 10–June 1	Apr. 1–June 1
Cornsalad	Feb. 1–Apr. 1	Feb. 15–Apr. 15	Mar. 1–May 1
Corn, sweet	Apr. 10–June 1	Apr. 25–June 15	May 10–June 15
Cress, upland	Mar. 10–Apr. 15	Mar. 20–May 1	Apr. 10–May 10
Cucumber	Apr. 20–June 1	May 1–June 15	May 15–June 15
Eggplant [1]	May 1–June 1	May 10–June 1	May 15–June 10
Endive	Mar. 15–Apr. 15	Mar. 25–Apr. 15	Apr. 1–May 1
Fennel, Florence	Mar. 15–Apr. 15	Mar. 25–Apr. 15	Apr. 1–May 1
Garlic	Feb. 20–Mar. 20	Mar. 10–Apr. 1	Mar. 15–Apr. 15
Horseradish [1]	Mar. 10–Apr. 10	Mar. 20–Apr. 20	Apr. 1–30
Kale	Mar. 10–Apr. 1	Mar. 20–Apr. 10	Apr. 1–20
Kohlrabi	Mar. 10–Apr. 10	Mar. 20–May 1	Apr. 1–May 10
Leek	Mar. 1–Apr. 1	Mar. 15–Apr. 15	Apr. 1–May 1
Lettuce, head [1]	Mar. 10–Apr. 1	Mar. 20–Apr. 15	Apr. 1–May 1
Lettuce, leaf	Mar. 15–May 15	Mar. 20–May 15	Apr. 1–June 1
Muskmelon	Apr. 20–June 1	May 1–June 15	May 15–June 15
Mustard	Mar. 10–Apr. 20	Mar. 20–May 1	Apr. 1–May 10
Okra	Apr. 20–June 15	May 1–June 1	May 10–June 1
Onion [1]	Mar. 1–Apr. 1	Mar. 15–Apr. 10	Apr. 1–May 1
Onion, seed	Mar. 1–Apr. 1	Mar. 15–Apr. 1	Mar. 15–Apr. 15
Onion, sets	Mar. 1–Apr. 1	Mar. 10–Apr. 1	Mar. 10–Apr. 10
Parsley	Mar. 10–Apr. 10	Mar. 20–Apr. 20	Apr. 1–May 1
Parsnip	Mar. 10–Apr. 10	Mar. 20–Apr. 20	Apr. 1–May 1
Peas, garden	Feb. 20–Mar. 20	Mar. 10–Apr. 10	Mar. 20–May 1
Peas, black-eye	May 1–July 1	May 10–June 15	May 15–June 1
Pepper [1]	May 1–June 1	May 10–June 1	May 15–June 10
Potato	Mar. 10–Apr. 1	Mar. 15–Apr. 10	Mar. 20–May 10
Radish	Mar. 1–May 1	Mar. 10–May 10	Mar. 20–May 10
Rhubarb [1]	Mar. 1–Apr. 1	Mar. 10–Apr. 10	Mar. 20–Apr. 15
Rutabaga			May 1–June 1
Salsify	Mar. 10–Apr. 15	Mar. 20–May 1	Apr. 1–May 15
Shallot	Mar. 1–Apr. 1	Mar. 15–Apr. 15	Apr. 1–May 1
Sorrel	Mar. 1–Apr. 15	Mar. 15–May 1	Apr. 1–May 15
Soybean	May 1–June 30	May 10–June 20	May 15–June 15
Spinach	Feb. 15–Apr. 1	Mar. 1–Apr. 15	Mar. 20–Apr. 20
Spinach, New Zealand	Apr. 20–June 1	May 1–June 15	May 1–June 15
Squash, summer	Apr. 20–June 1	May 1–June 15	May 1–30
Sweetpotato	May 1–June 1	May 10–June 10	May 20–June 10
Tomato	Apr. 20–June 1	May 5–June 10	May 10–June 15
Turnip	Mar. 1–June 1	Mar. 10–Apr. 1	Mar. 20–May 1
Watermelon	Apr. 20–June 1	May 1–June 15	May 15–June 15

[1] Plants.
[2] Generally fall-planted (table 5).

spring planting of vegetables in the open—Continued

in which average date of last freeze is—

May 10	May 20	May 30	June 10
Mar. 10–Apr. 30 ____	Apr. 20–May 15 ____	May 1–June 1 _____	May 15–June 1.
May 25–June 15 ___	----------------------	----------------------	
May 10–June 30 ___	May–15–June 30 ___	May 25–June 15 ___	
Apr. 15–June 15 ___	Apr. 25–June 15 ___	May 1–June 15 ____	May 15–June 15.
Apr. 15–June 1 ____	May 1–June 15 ____	May 10–June 10 ___	May 20–June 10.
Apr. 15–June 1 ____	May 1–June 15 ____	May 10–June 10 ___	May 20–June 10.
Apr. 1–May 15 _____	May 1–June 15 ____	May 10–June 15 ___	May 20–June 1.
Apr. 1–May 15 _____	May 1–June 15 ____	May 10–June 15 ___	May 20–June 1.
Apr. 20–June 15 ___	May 1–June 1 _____	May 10–June 1 ___	May 20–June 1.
Apr. 15–May 15 ____	May 10–June 15 ___	May 20–June 1 ____	June 1–June 15.
Apr. 20–June 15 ___	May 10–June 15 ___	May 20–June 1 ____	June 1–June 15.
Apr. 20–June 15 ___	May 10–June 15 ___	May 20–June 1 ____	June 1–June 15.
Apr. 1–May 1 _____	Apr. 15–May 15 ____	May 1–June 1 _____	May 15–June 1.
June 1–20 _____	June 1–15 _____	June 1–15 _____	June 1–15.
Apr. 15–June 1 ____	May 1–June 1 _____	May 10–June 1 ___	May 20–June 1.
Apr. 1–June 1 _____	Apr. 15–June 1 ____	May 1–June 15 ____	May 15–June 15.
May 10–June 1 ___	May 15–June 1 ____	May 20–June 1 ____	
Apr. 20–May 20 ____	May 1–June 1 _____	May 15–June 1 ___	May 15–June 15.
May 20–June 15 ___	June 1–15 _____	----------------------	
May 20–June 15 ___	June 1–15 _____	----------------------	
Apr. 15–May 15 ___	May 1–30 _____	May 1–30 _____	May 15–June 1.
Apr. 15–May 15 ____	May 1–30 _____	May 1–30 _____	May 15–June 1.
Apr. 1–May 1 _____	Apr. 15–May 15 ____	May 1–30 _____	May 15–June 1.
Apr. 15–May 15 ____	Apr. 20–May 20 ____	May 1–30 _____	May 15–June 1.
Apr. 10–May 1 ____	Apr. 20–May 10 ____	May 1–30 _____	May 15–June 1.
Apr. 10–May 15 ____	Apr. 20–May 20 ____	May 1–30 _____	May 15–June 1.
Apr. 15–May 15 ____	May 1–May 20 _____	May 1–15 _____	May 1–15.
Apr. 15–May 15 ____	May 1–June 30 ____	May 10–June 30 ___	May 20–June 30.
Apr. 15–June 15 ___	May 1–June 30 ____	May 10–June 30 ___	May 20–June 30.
June 1–June 15 ____	----------------------	----------------------	
Apr. 15–June 1 ____	May 1–June 30 ____	May 10–June 30 ___	May 20–June 30.
May 20–June 10 ___	June 1–20 _____	----------------------	
Apr. 10–May 1 ____	Apr. 20–May 15 ____	May 1–30 _____	May 10–June 10.
Apr. 1–May 1 _____	Apr. 20–May 15 ____	May 1–30 _____	May 10–June 10.
Apr. 10–May 1 ____	Apr. 20–May 15 ____	May 1–30 _____	May 10–June 10.
Apr. 15–May 15 ____	May 1–20 _____	May 10–June 1 ____	May 20–June 10.
Apr. 15–May 15 ___	May 1–20 _____	May 10–June 1 ____	May 20–June 10.
Apr. 1–May 15 _____	Apr. 15–June 1 ____	May 1–June 15 ____	May 10–June 15.
May 20–June 10 ___	May 25–June 15 ___	June 1–15 _____	
Apr. 1–June 1 _____	Apr. 15–June 15 ___	May 1–June 15 ____	May 15–June 1.
Apr. 1–June 1 _____	Apr. 15–June 15 ___	May 1–June 15 ____	May 15–June 1.
Apr. 1–May 1 _____	Apr. 15–May 10 ____	May 1–20 _____	May 15–June 1.
May 1–June 1 _____	May 1–20 _____	May 10–20 _____	May 20–June 1.
Apr. 15–June 1 ____	May 1–June 1 _____	May 10–June 1 ____	May 20–June 1.
Apr. 10–May 1 _____	Apr. 20–May 10 ____	May 1–June 1 _____	May 10–June 1.
Apr. 15–June 1 ____	May 1–June 1 _____	May 10–June 10 ___	May 10–June 10.
May 25–June 10 ___	----------------------	----------------------	
Apr. 1–June 15 ____	Apr. 10–June 15 ___	Apr. 20–June 15 ___	May 1–June 15.
May 10–June 15 ___	May 20–June 15 ___	June 1–15 _____	
May 10–June 10 ___	May 20–June 15 ___	June 1–20 _____	June 10–20.
----------------------	May 25–June 15 ___	June 5–20 _____	June 15–30.
May 15–June 10 ___	Apr. 15–June 1 ____	May 1–June 15 ____	May 15–June 15.
Apr. 1–June 1 _____	June 15–July 1 ___	----------------------	
June 1–June 15 ____			

TABLE 5.—*Latest dates, and range of dates, for safe fall planting of vegetables in the open*

Crop	Planting dates for localities in which average dates of first freeze is—					
	Aug. 30	Sept. 10	Sept. 20	Sept. 30	Oct. 10	Oct. 20
Asparagus [1]				June 1-15	Oct. 20-Nov. 15	Nov. 1-Dec. 15.
Beans, lima				June 1-15	June 1-15	June 15-30.
Beans, snap	May 15-June 15	May 15-June 15	June 1-July 1	June 1-July 10	June 1-July 20	July 1-Aug. 1.
Beet	May 1-June 1	May 1-June 1	June 1-July 1	June 1-July 10	June 15-July 25	July 1-Aug. 5.
Broccoli, sprouting	May 1-June 1	May 1-June 1	May 1-June 15	June 1-30	June 15-July 15	July 1-Aug. 1.
Brussels sprouts	May 1-June 1	May 1-June 1	May 1-June 15	June 1-30	June 15-July 15	July 1-Aug. 1.
Cabbage [1]	May 1-June 1	May 1-June 1	May 1-June 15	June 1-July 10	June 1-July 15	July 1-20.
Cabbage, Chinese	May 15-June 15	May 15-June 15	June 1-July 1	June 1-July 15	June 15-Aug. 1	July 15-Aug. 15.
Carrot	May 15-June 15	May 15-June 15	June 1-July 1	June 1-July 10	June 1-July 20	June 15-Aug. 1.
Cauliflower [1]	May 1-June 1	May 1-July 1	May 1-July 1	May 10-July 15	June 1-July 25	July 1-Aug. 5.
Celery [1] and celeriac	May 1-June 1	May 15-June 15	May 15-July 1	June 1-July 5	June 1-July 15	June 1-Aug. 1.
Chard	May 15-June 15	May 15-July 1	June 1-July 1	June 1-July 5	June 1-July 20	June 1-Aug. 1.
Chervil and chives	May 10-June 10	May 1-June 15	May 15-June 15	(2)	(2)	(2)
Chicory, witloof	May 15-June 15	May 15-June 15	May 15-June 15	June 1-July 1	June 1-July 1	June 15-July 15.
Collards [1]	May 15-June 15	May 15-June 15	May 15-June 15	June 15-July 15	July 1-Aug. 1	July 15-Aug. 15.
Cornsalad	May 15-June 15	May 15-July 1	June 15-Aug. 1	July 15-Sept. 1	Aug. 15-Sept. 15	Sept. 1-Oct. 15.
Corn, sweet			June 1-July 1	June 1-July 1	June 1-July 10	June 1-July 20.
Cress, upland	May 15-June 15	May 15-July 1	June 15-Aug. 1	July 15-Sept. 1	Aug. 15-Sept. 15	Sept. 1-Oct. 15.
Cucumber			June 1-15	June 1-July 1	June 1-July 1	June 1-July 15.
Eggplant [1]				May 20-June 10	May 15-June 15	June 1-July 1.
Endive	June 1-July 1	June 1-July 1	June 15-July 15	June 15-Aug. 1	July 1-Aug. 15	July 15-Sept. 1.
Fennel, Florence	May 15-June 15	May 15-July 15	June 1-July 1	June 1-July 1	June 15-July 15	June 15-Aug. 1.
Garlic	(2)	(2)	(2)	(2)	(2)	(2)
Horseradish [1]	(2)	(2)	(2)	(2)	(2)	(2)
Kale	May 15-June 15	May 15-June 15	June 1-July 1	June 15-July 15	July 1-Aug. 1	July 15-Aug. 15.

Kohlrabi	May 15–June 15	June 1–July 1	June 1–July 15	June 15–July 15	July 1–Aug. 1	July 15–Aug. 15.
Leek [1]	May 1–June 1	May 1–June 1	(2)	(2)	(2)	(2)
Lettuce, head [1]	May 15–July 1	May 15–July 15	June 1–July 15	June 15–Aug. 1	July 15–Aug. 1	Aug. 1–30.
Lettuce, leaf	May 15–July 15	May 15–July 15	June 1–Aug. 1	June 1–Aug. 1	July 15–Sept. 1	July 15–Sept. 1.
Muskmelon		May 15–July 15	June 1–June 20	May 15–June 15	June 1–June 15	June 15–July 20.
Mustard	May 15–July 15	May 15–July 15	May 15–June 15	June 15–Aug. 1	July 15–Aug. 15	Aug. 1–Sept. 1.
Okra [1]			June 1–20	June 1–July 1	June 1–July 15	June 1–Aug. 1.
Onion [1]	May 1–June 10	May 1–June 10	(2)	(2)	(2)	(2)
Onion, seed	May 1–June 1	May 1–June 1	(2)	(2)	(2)	(2)
Onion, sets	May 1–June 10	May 1–June 10	(2)	(2)	(2)	(2)
Parsley	May 15–June 15	May 15–June 15	May 15–July 1	June 1–July 15	June 15–Aug. 1	July 15–Aug. 15.
Parsnip	May 1–June 1	May 1–June 1	May 15–June 15	June 1–July 1	June 1–July 10	(2)
Peas, garden	May 15–June 15	May 15–June 15	May 15–July 1	June 1–July 15	(2)	(2)
Peas, black-eye	May 10–July 1	May 15–June 15	June 1–June 20	June 1–June 20	June 1–July 1	June 1–July 1.
Pepper [1]		May 15–June 15	May 15–June 15	May 15–June 15	June 1–July 1	June 1–July 10.
Potato	May 1–June 15	May 1–June 15	May 1–June 15	May 15–June 15	May 15–June 15	June 15–July 15.
Radish	May 1–July 15	May 1–Aug. 1	June 1–Aug. 15	July 1–Sept. 1	July 15–Sept. 15	Aug. 1–Oct. 1.
Rhubarb [1]	Sept. 1–Oct. 15	Sept. 1–Oct. 15	Sept. 15–Oct. 15	Sept. 15–Nov. 1	Oct. 15–Nov. 15	Oct. 15–Dec. 1.
Rutabaga	May 15–June 15	May 15–June 15	May 15–June 20	June 1–July 1	June 15–July 15	July 10–20.
Salsify	May 15–June 1	May 15–June 15	May 20–June 20	June 1–20	June 1–July 1	June 1–July 1.
Shallot	(2)	(2)	(2)	(2)	(2)	(2)
Sorrel	May 15–June 15	May 15–July 1	June 1–July 15	July 1–Aug. 1	July 1–Aug. 1	July 15–Aug. 15.
Soybean	May 15–June 15	June 1–July 1	June 1–July 1	May 25–June 10	June 1–25	June 1–July 5.
Spinach	May 15–July 1	June 1–July 15	June 1–Aug. 1	July 1–Aug. 15	Aug. 1–Sept. 1	Aug. 20–Sept. 10.
Spinach, New Zealand		June 1–July 15	June 1–Aug. 1	June 1–Aug. 1	June 15–July 15	June 1–Aug. 1.
Squash, summer	June 10–20	June 1–20	May 15–July 1	May 15–July 1	June 1–July 1	June 1–July 20.
Squash, winter			June 10–20	May 20–June 10	June 1–July 1	June 1–July 1.
Sweetpotato [1]				May 20–June 10	May 20–June 10	June 1–15.
Tomato [1]	June 20–30	June 1–20	June 1–20	June 1–20	June 1–20	June 1–July 1.
Turnip	May 15–June 15	June 1–July 1	June 1–July 15	June 1–Aug. 1	July 1–Aug. 1	July 15–Aug. 15.
Watermelon		May 15–June 15	May 1–June 15	May 15–June 1	June 1–June 15	June 15–July 20.

[1] Plants.

[2] Generally spring-planted (table 4).

TABLE 5.—*Latest dates, and range of dates, for safe fall planting of vegetables in the open*—Continued

Crop	Planting dates for localities in which average date of first freeze is—					
	Oct. 30	Nov. 10	Nov. 20	Nov. 30	Dec. 10	Dec. 20
Asparagus [1]	Nov. 15–Jan. 1	Dec. 1–Jan. 1				
Beans, lima	July 1–Aug. 1	July 1–Aug. 15	July 15–Sept. 1	Aug. 1–Sept. 15	Sept. 1–30	Sept. 1–Oct. 1.
Beans, snap	July 1–Aug. 15	July 1–Sept. 1	July 1–Sept. 10	Aug. 15–Sept. 20	Sept. 1–30	Sept. 1–Nov. 1.
Beet	Aug. 1–Sept. 1	Aug. 1–Oct. 1	Sept. 1–Dec. 1	Sept. 1–Dec. 15	Sept. 1–Dec. 31	Sept. 1–Dec. 31.
Broccoli, sprouting	July 1–Aug. 15	Aug. 1–Sept. 1	Aug. 1–Sept. 15	Aug. 1–Oct. 1	Aug. 1–Nov. 1	Sept. 1–Dec. 31.
Brussels sprouts	July 1–Aug. 15	Aug. 1–Sept. 1	Aug. 1–Sept. 15	Aug. 1–Oct. 1	Aug. 1–Nov. 1	Sept. 1–Dec. 31.
Cabbage [1]	Aug. 1–Sept. 1	Sept. 1–15	Sept. 1–Dec. 1	Sept. 1–Dec. 31	Sept. 1–Dec. 31	Sept. 1–Dec. 31.
Cabbage, Chinese	Aug. 1–Sept. 15	Aug. 15–Oct. 1	Sept. 1–Oct. 15	Sept. 1–Nov. 1	Sept. 1–Nov. 15	Sept. 1–Dec. 1.
Carrot	July 1–Aug. 15	Aug. 1–Sept. 1	Sept. 1–Nov. 1	Sept. 15–Dec. 1	Sept. 15–Dec. 1	Sept. 15–Dec. 1.
Cauliflower [1]	July 15–Aug. 15	Aug. 1–Sept. 1	Aug. 1–Sept. 15	Sept. 15–Dec. 1	Sept. 15–Dec. 1	Sept. 15–Dec. 1.
Celery [1] and celeriac	June 15–Aug. 15	July 1–Aug. 15	July 15–Sept. 1	Aug. 15–Oct. 10	Sept. 1–Oct. 20	Sept. 15–Nov. 1.
Chard	June 1–Sept. 10	June 1–Sept. 15	June 1–Oct. 1	Aug. 1–Dec. 1	Sept. 1–Dec. 31	Oct. 1–Dec. 31.
Chervil and chives	[2]	[2]	Nov. 1–Dec. 31	Nov. 1–Dec. 31	Nov. 1–Dec. 31	June 1–Dec. 31.
Chicory, witloof	July 1–Aug. 10	July 10–Aug. 20	July 20–Sept. 1	Aug. 15–Sept. 30	Aug. 15–Oct. 15	Aug. 15–Oct. 15.
Collards [1]	Aug. 1–Sept. 15	Aug. 15–Oct. 1	Aug. 25–Nov. 1	Sept. 1–Dec. 1	Sept. 1–Dec. 31	Sept. 1–Dec. 31.
Cornsalad	Sept. 15–Nov. 1	Oct. 1–Dec. 1	Oct. 1–Dec. 1	Oct. 1–Dec. 31	Oct. 1–Dec. 31	Oct. 1–Dec. 31.
Corn, sweet	June 1–Aug. 15	June 1–Aug. 15	June 1–Sept. 1	June 1–Sept. 1		
Cress, upland	Sept. 15–Nov. 1	Oct. 1–Dec. 1	Oct. 1–Dec. 1	Oct. 1–Dec. 31	Oct. 1–Dec. 31	Oct. 1–Dec. 31.
Cucumber	June 1–Aug. 1	June 1–Aug. 15	June 1–Aug. 15	June 1–Aug. 15	Aug. 15–Oct. 1	Aug. 15–Oct. 1.
Eggplant [1]	June 1–July 1	June 1–July 15	June 1–Aug. 1	July 1–Sept. 1	Aug. 1–Sept. 30	Aug. 1–Sept. 30.
Endive	July 15–Aug. 15	Aug. 1–Sept. 1	Sept. 1–Oct. 1	Sept. 1–Nov. 15	Sept. 1–Dec. 31	Sept. 1–Dec. 31.
Fennel, Florence	July 1–Aug. 15	July 15–Aug. 15	Aug. 15–Sept. 15	Sept. 1–Nov. 15	Sept. 1–Dec. 1	Sept. 1–Dec. 1.
Garlic	[2]	Aug. 1–Oct. 1	Aug. 15–Oct. 15	Sept. 1–Nov. 15	Sept. 15–Nov. 15	Sept. 15–Nov. 15.
Horseradish [1]	[2]	[2]	[2]	[2]	[2]	[2]
Kale	July 15–Sept. 1	Aug. 1–Sept. 15	Aug. 15–Oct. 15	Sept. 1–Dec. 1	Sept. 1–Dec. 31	Sept. 1–Dec. 31.

Kohlrabi	Aug. 1–Sept. 1	Aug. 15–Sept. 15	Sept. 1–Oct. 15	Sept. 1–Dec. 1	Sept. 15–Dec. 31	Sept. 1–Dec. 31.
Leek	(2)	(2)	Sept. 1–Nov. 1	Sept. 1–Nov. 1	Sept. 1–Nov. 1	Sept. 15–Nov. 1
Lettuce, head [1]	Aug. 1–Sept. 15	Aug. 15–Oct. 15	Sept. 1–Nov. 1	Sept. 1–Dec. 1	Sept. 15–Dec. 31	Sept. 15–Dec. 31.
Lettuce, leaf	Aug. 15–Oct. 15	Aug. 25–Oct. 1	Sept. 1–Nov. 1	Sept. 1–Dec. 1	Sept. 15–Dec. 31	Sept. 15–Dec. 31.
Muskmelon	July 1–July 15	July 15–July 30				
Mustard	Aug. 15–Oct. 15	Aug. 15–Nov. 1	Sept. 1–Dec. 1	Sept. 1–Dec. 1	Sept. 1–Dec. 1	Sept. 15–Dec. 1.
Okra	June 1–Aug. 10	June 1–Aug. 20	June 1–Sept. 10	June 1–Sept. 20	Aug. 1–Oct. 1.	Aug. 1–Oct. 1.
Onion [1]		Sept. 1–Oct. 15	Oct. 1–Dec. 31	Oct. 1–Dec. 31	Oct. 1–Dec. 31	Oct. 1–Dec. 31.
Onion, seed			Oct. 1–Dec. 1	Sept. 1–Nov. 15	Sept. 15–Nov. 1	Sept. 15–Nov. 1.
Onion, sets		Oct. 1–Dec. 1		Nov. 1–Dec. 31	Nov. 1–Dec. 31	Nov. 1–Dec. 31.
Parsley	Aug. 1–Sept. 15	Sept. 1–Nov. 15	Aug. 1–Sept. 1	Sept. 1–Dec. 1	Sept. 1–Dec. 1	Sept. 1–Dec. 1.
Parsnip	(2)		Oct. 1–Dec. 1	Oct. 1–Dec. 31	Oct. 1–Dec. 31	Oct. 1–Dec. 31.
Peas, garden	Aug. 1–Sept. 15	Sept. 1–Nov. 1	July 1–Sept. 1	July 1–Sept. 1	July 1–Sept. 10	July 1–Sept. 20.
Peas, black-eye	June 1–Aug. 1	June 15–Aug. 15	June 1–Aug. 15	June 1–Sept. 1	July 1–Sept. 1	Aug. 15–Oct. 1.
Pepper [1]	June 1–July 20	June 1–Aug. 1	June 1–Aug. 15	June 15–Sept. 1	Aug. 15–Oct. 1	Aug. 1–Sept. 15.
Potato	July 20–Aug. 10	July 25–Aug. 20	Aug. 10–Sept. 15	Aug. 1–Sept. 15	Aug. 1–Sept. 15	Oct. 1–Dec. 31.
Radish	Aug. 15–Oct. 15	Sept. 1–Nov. 15	Sept. 1–Dec. 1	Sept. 1–Dec. 31	Sept. 1–Dec. 31	Oct. 1–Dec. 31.
Rhubarb [1]	Nov. 1–Dec. 1					Oct. 15–Nov. 15.
Rutabaga	July 15–Aug. 1	July 15–July 20	July 15–Aug. 15	Aug. 15–Sept. 30	Aug. 15–Oct. 15	Sept. 1–Oct. 31.
Salsify	June 1–July 10	June 15–July 20	June 15–July 20	Aug. 15–Oct. 15	Sept. 15–Oct. 15	Sept. 15–Nov. 1.
Shallot	(2)	Aug. 1–Oct. 1	Aug. 1–Oct. 1	Aug. 15–Oct. 15	Sept. 1–Dec. 15	Sept. 1–Dec. 31.
Sorrel	Aug. 1–Sept. 15	Aug. 15–Oct. 15	June 1–July 25	June 1–July 30	June 1–July 30	June 1–July 30.
Soybean	June 1–July 15	June 1–July 25	June 1–July 30	June 1–July 30	June 1–July 30	
Spinach	Sept. 1–Oct. 1	Sept. 15–Nov. 1	Sept. 15–Nov. 1	Oct. 1–Dec. 1	Oct. 1–Dec. 1	Oct. 1–Dec. 31.
Spinach, New Zealand	June 1–Aug. 1	June 1–Aug. 15	June 1–Aug. 15	June 1–Aug. 15	June 1–Aug. 15	
Squash, summer	June 1–Aug. 1	June 1–Aug. 10	June 1–Aug. 20	June 1–Aug. 20	July 15–Aug. 15	June 1–Oct. 1.
Squash, winter	June 10–July 10	June 20–July 20	June 20–July 20	July 1–Aug. 1	July 1–Aug. 1	Aug. 1–Sept. 1.
Sweetpotato	June 1–15	June 1–July 1	June 1–July 1	June 1–July 1	June 1–July 1	June 1–July 1.
Tomato	June 1–July 1	June 1–July 15	June 1–July 15	June 1–Aug. 1	June 1–Aug. 1	Sept. 1–Nov. 1.
Turnip	Aug. 1–Sept. 15	Sept. 1–Oct. 15	Sept. 1–Nov. 15	Sept. 1–Nov. 15	Sept. 1–Nov. 1	Oct. 1–Dec. 31.
Watermelon	July 1–July 15	July 15–July 30				

[1] Plants.
[2] Generally spring-planted (table 4).

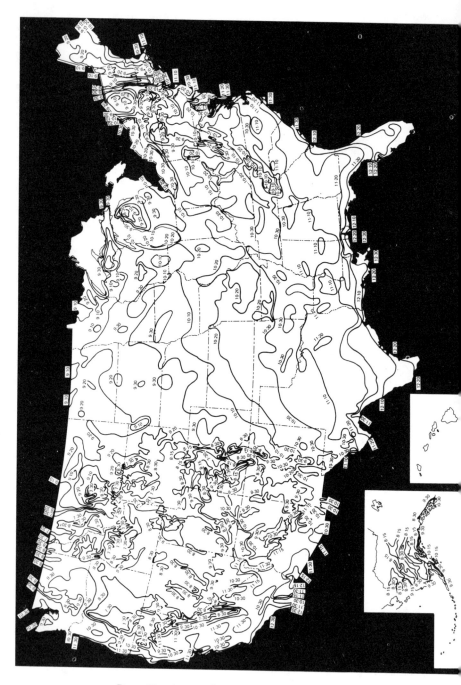

Figure 13.—Average dates of the first killing frost in fall.

CARING FOR THE GARDEN

Watering

In most areas the garden requires a moisture supply equivalent to about an inch of rain a week during the growing season for best plant growth. It requires roughly that amount of watering a week to maintain good production if the moisture stored in the soil becomes depleted and no rain falls over periods of weeks. An inch of rain is equivalent to about 28,000 gallons on an acre, or 900 gallons on a 30- by 50-foot garden.

It is much better to give the garden a good soaking about once a week than to water it sparingly more often. Light sprinklings at frequent intervals do little, if any, good. The best way to apply water, when the soil and slope are suitable, is to run it the length of furrows between the rows until the soil is well soaked. If the soil is very sandy or the surface too irregular for the furrow method, sprinklers or porous irrigating hose must be used.

Controlling Weeds

Weeds rob cultivated plants of water, nutrients, and light. Some weeds harbor diseases, insects, and nematodes that reinfest garden crops in succeeding years.

As soon as the soil can be properly worked after each rain or irrigation, it should be thoroughly hoed or cultivated to kill weeds that have sprouted and to leave the surface in a loose, friable condition to absorb later rainfall. The primary value of hoeing or cultivating is weed control. This cultivation should be shallow so as to avoid injuring the vegetable plant roots that lie near the surface. Although it is desirable to keep the surface soil loose, there is little to be gained by hoeing or cultivating oftener than necessary to keep weeds out of the garden.

In small gardens, weeds can be controlled with black polyethylene mulch (fig. 14) supplemented by hand weeding such as pulling, hoeing, and wheel hoeing. Mulching vegetable crops with organic material also is a common practice in small gardens.

The best organic mulches are partially decomposed hay, straw, or grass clippings. The mulch should be applied 4 to 6 inches deep when the plants are about 6 inches tall. Cabbage, tomato, and other transplants usually are tall enough soon after they are set in the garden. Before applying mulch, hoe out all small weeds. Not only does mulch control weeds, it also conserves moisture, keeps the soil from packing, and increases the humus necessary for vigorous plant growth.

Controlling Diseases and Insects

Garden crops are subject to attack by a number of diseases and insects. Preventive measures are best, but if an attack occurs and the gardener is not familiar with the insect or disease and the proper treatment to protect his crop, he is advised to consult the county agent or write

PN-2623

Figure 14.—Black plastic film conserves moisture, controls weeds, warms the soil, and hastens maturity of vegetable crops.

immediately to his experiment station. The
United States Department of Agriculture and
many of the States have publications containing the necessary information on garden diseases and insects, and these can be procured
free upon request. Detailed information can be
found in USDA Home and Garden Bulletin 46,
Insects and Diseases of Vegetables in the Home
Garden.

Among the most important disease-control
measures are the use of disease-free seeds and
plants, and the use of disease-resistant varieties. Great progress has been made within recent years in the development of varieties that
are resistant to certain diseases.

GROWING SPECIFIC VEGETABLES

Perennial Vegetables

The larger vegetables gardens need a number
of perennials. Asparagus, horseradish, and
rhubarb are the most important, but chives,
bottom multiplier onions, and some of the
flavoring and condiment plants, chiefly sage
and mint, are also desirable. Unfortunately,
asparagus, horseradish, and rhubarb are not
adapted to conditions in the lower South.

All the perennial crops should be grouped together along one side of the garden, where they
will not interfere with work on the annual
crops.

Asparagus

Asparagus is among the earliest of spring

vegetables. An area about 20 feet square, or a row 50 to 75 feet long, will supply plenty of fresh asparagus for a family of five or six persons, provided the soil is well enriched and the plants are given good attention. More must be planted if a supply is to be canned or frozen.

Asparagus does best where winters are cold enough to freeze the ground to a depth of a few inches at least. In many southern areas the plants make a weak growth, producing small shoots. Elevation has some effect, but, in general, the latitude of south-central Georgia is the southern limit of profitable culture.

The crop can be grown on almost any well-drained, fertile soil, and there is little possibility of having the soil too rich, especially through the use of manure. Loosen the soil far down, either by subsoil plowing or by deep spading before planting. Throw the topsoil aside and spade manure, leafmold, rotted leaves, or peat into the subsoil to a depth of 14 to 16 inches; then mix from 5 to 10 pounds of a complete fertilizer into each 75-foot row or 20-foot bed.

When the soil is ready for planting, the bottom of the trench should be about 6 inches below the natural level of the soil. After the crowns are set and covered to a depth of an inch or two, gradually work the soil into the trench around the plants during the first season. When set in beds, asparagus plants should be at least 1½ feet apart each way; when set in rows, they should be about 1½ feet apart with the rows from 4 to 5 feet apart.

Asparagus plants, or crowns, are grown from seed. The use of 1-year-old plants only is recommended. These should have a root spread of at least 15 inches, and larger ones are better. The home gardener will usually find it best to buy his plants from a grower who has a good strain of a recognized variety. Mary Washington and Waltham Washington are good varieties that have the added merit of being rust resistant. Waltham Washington is an improved strain of Mary Washington. It contains very little of the purple over-cast predominant in the Mary Washington, is a high yielder, and has good green color clear into the ground line. In procuring asparagus crowns, it is always well to be sure that they have not been allowed to dry out.

Clean cultivation encourages vigorous growth; it behooves the gardener to keep his asparagus clean from the start. In a large farm garden, with long rows, most of the work can be done with a horse-drawn cultivator or a garden tractor. In a small garden, where the rows are short or the asparagus is planted in beds, however, hand work is necessary.

For a 75-foot row, an application of manure and 6 to 8 pounds of a high-grade complete fertilizer, once each year, is recommended. Manure and fertilizer may be applied either before or after the cutting season.

Remove no shoots the year the plants are set in the permanent bed and keep the cutting period short the year after setting. Remove all shoots during the cutting season in subsequent years (fig. 15). Cease cutting about July 1 to 10 and let the tops grow. In the autumn, remove and burn the dead tops.

Asparagus rust and asparagus beetles are the chief enemies of the crop.

PN–2624
Figure 15.—Asparagus shoots ready to be cut.

Horseradish

Horseradish is adapted to the north-temperate regions of the United States, but not to the South, except possibly in the high altitudes.

Any good soil, except possibly the lightest sands and heaviest clays, will grow horseradish, but it does best on a deep, rich, moist loam that is well supplied with organic matter. Avoid shallow soil; it produces rough, prongy roots. Mix organic matter with the soil a few months before the plants or cuttings are set. Some fertilizer may be used at the time of planting and more during the subsequent seasons. A top dressing of organic matter each spring is advisable.

Horseradish is propagated either by crowns or by root cuttings. In propagating by crowns a portion of an old plant consisting of a piece of root and crown buds is merely lifted and planted in a new place. Root cuttings are pieces of older roots 6 to 8 inches long and of the thickness of a lead pencil. They may be saved when preparing the larger roots for grating, or they may be purchased from seedsmen. A trench 4 or 5 inches deep is opened with a hoe and the root cuttings are placed at an angle with their tops near the surface of the ground. Plants from these cuttings usually make good roots the first year. As a rule, the plants in the home garden are allowed to grow from year to year, and portions of the roots are removed as needed. Pieces of roots and crowns remaining in the soil are usually sufficient to reestablish the plants.

There is very little choice in the matter of varieties of horseradish. Be sure, however, to obtain good healthy planting stock of a strain that is giving good results in the area where it is being grown. New Bohemian is perhaps the best known sort sold by American seedsmen.

Rhubarb

Rhubarb thrives best in regions having cool moist summers and winters cold enough to freeze the ground to a depth of several inches. It is not adapted to most parts of the South, but in certain areas of higher elevation it does fairly well. A few hills along the garden fence will supply all that a family can use.

Any deep, well-drained, fertile soil is suitable

for rhubarb. Spade the soil or plow it to a depth of 12 to 16 inches and mix in rotted manure, leafmold, decayed hardwood leaves, sods, or other form of organic matter. The methods of soil preparation suggested for asparagus are suitable for rhubarb. As rhubarb is planted in hills 3 to 4 feet apart, however, it is usually sufficient to prepare each hill separately.

Rhubarb plants may be started from seed and transplanted, but seedlings vary from the parent plant. The usual method of starting the plants is to obtain pieces of crowns from established hills and set them in prepared hills. Top-dress the planting with a heavy application of organic matter in either early spring or late fall. Organic matter applied over the hills during early spring greatly hastens growth, or forces the plant.

A pound of complete commercial fertilizer high in nitrogen applied around each hill every year insures an abundant supply of plant food. The plants can be mulched with green grass or weeds.

Remove seedstalks as soon as they form. No leaf stems should be harvested before the second year and but few until the third. Moreover, the harvest season must be largely confined to early spring. The hills should be divided and reset every 7 or 8 years. Otherwise, they become too thick and produce only slender stems.

Crimson, Red Valentine, MacDonald, Canada Red, and Victoria are standard varieties. Use only the leafstalk as a food. **Rhubarb leaves contain injurious substances, including oxalic acid. Never use them for food.**

Sorrel

Sorrel is a perennial that is usually started from seeds. It requires a rich, mellow, well-drained soil. Rows may be of any convenient distance apart. Thin the plants to about 8 inches apart in the rows. If the leaves alone are gathered and the plants are cultivated to prevent the growth of weeds, a planting should last 3 or 4 years. French Broad Leaf is a well-known variety.

Greens

Greens are usually the leaves and leaf stems of immature plants, which in their green state are boiled for food. Young, tender branches of certain plants, New Zealand spinach, for example, are also used this way. All the plants treated here as greens except New Zealand spinach are hardy vegetables, most of them adapted to fall sowing and winter culture over the entire South and in the more temperate parts of the North. Their culture may be extended more widely in the North by growing them with some protection, such as mulching or frames.

Chard

Chard, or Swiss chard (fig. 16), is a type of beet that has been developed for its tops instead of its roots. Crop after crop of the outer leaves may be harvested without injuring the plant. Only one planting is necessary, and a row 30 to 40 feet long will supply a family for the entire summer. Each seed cluster contains several seeds, and fairly wide spacing of the seeds facilitates thinning. The culture of chard is practically the same as that of beets, but the plants grow larger and need to be thinned to at least 6 inches apart in the row. Chard needs a rich, mellow soil, and it is sensitive to soil acidity.

Witloof Chicory

Witloof chicory, or French endive, is grown for both roots and tops. It is a hardy plant, not especially sensitive to heat or cold. It does, however, need a deep, rich, loamy soil without too much organic matter. The tops are sometimes harvested while young. The roots are lifted in

PN–2625

Figure 16.—Swiss chard is especially suitable for hot-weather culture.

autumn and placed in a box or bed of moist soil in a warm cellar for forcing. They must be covered with a few inches of sand. Under this covering the leaves form in a solid head, known on the market as witloof.

The culture of chicory is simple. Sow the seeds in spring or early summer in drills about 18 inches apart. Later, thin the plants to 6 or 8 inches apart in the rows. If sown too early the plants shoot to seed and are worthless for forcing. The kind known as witloof is most generally used.

Collards

Collards are grown and used about like cabbage. They withstand heat better than other members of the cabbage group, and are well liked in the South for both summer and winter use. Collards do not form a true head, but a large rosette of leaves, which may be blanched by tying together.

Cornsalad

Cornsalad is also known as lamb's-lettuce and fetticus. Sow the seed in early spring in drills and cultivate the plants the same as lettuce or mustard. For an extra early crop, plant the seed in the autumn and cover the plants lightly through the winter. In the Southern States the covering is not necessary, and the plants are ready for use in February and March. The leaves are frequently used in their natural green state, but they may be blanched by covering the rows with anything that will exclude light.

Kale

Kale, or borecole, is hardy and lives over winter in latitudes as far north as northern Maryland and southern Pennsylvania and in other areas where similar winter conditions prevail. It is also resistant to heat and may be grown in summer. Its real merit, however, is a cool-weather greens.

Kale is a member of the cabbage family. The best garden varieties are low-growing, spreading plants, with thick, more or less crinkled leaves (fig. 17). Vates Blue Curled, Dwarf Blue Scotch, and Siberian are well-known garden varieties.

PN–2626

Figure 17.—Kale, a hardy green, is mulched here with spoiled hay.

No other plant is so well adapted to fall sowing throughout a wide area of both North and South or in areas characterized by winters of moderate severity. Kale may well follow some such early-season vegetable as green beans, potatoes, or peas.

In the autumn the seed may be broadcast very thinly and then lightly raked into the soil. Except for spring sowings, made when weeds are troublesome, sow kale in rows 18 to 24 inches apart and later thin the plants to about a foot apart.

Kale may be harvested either by cutting the entire plant or by taking the larger leaves while young. Old kale is tough and stringy.

Mustard

Mustard grows well on almost any good soil. As the plants require but a short time to reach the proper stage for use, frequent sowings are recommended. Sow the seeds thickly in drills as early as possible in the spring or, for late use, in September or October. The forms of Indian mustard, the leaves of which are often curled and frilled, are generally used. Southern Curled and Green Wave are common sorts.

Spinach

Spinach is a hardy cool-weather plant that withstands winter conditions in the South. In most of the North, spinach is primarily an early-spring and late-fall crop, but in some areas, where summer temperatures are mild, it may be grown continuously from early spring until late fall. It should be emphasized that summer and winter culture of spinach is possible only where moderate temperatures prevail.

Spinach will grow on almost any well-drained, fertile soil where sufficient moisture is available. It is very sensitive to acid soil. If a soil test shows the need, apply lime to the part of the garden used for spinach, regardless of the treatment given the rest of the area.

The application of 100 pounds of rotted manure and 3 to 4 pounds of commercial fertilizer to each 100 square feet of land is suitable for spinach in the home garden. Broadcast both

manure and fertilizer and work them in before
sowing the seed.

Long Standing Bloomsdale is perhaps the
most popular variety seeded in spring. It is
attractive, grows quickly, is very productive,
and will stand for a moderate length of time
before going to seed. Virginia Savoy and Hybrid No. 7 are valuable varieties for fall planting, as they are resistant to yellows, or blight.
Hybrid No. 7 is also resistant to downy mildew
(blue mold). These two varieties are very cold-
hardy but are not suitable for the spring crop,
as they produce seedstalks too early. For horse
or tractor cultivation, the rows of the garden
should be not less than 24 inches apart; when
land is plentiful they may be 30 inches apart.
For wheel-hoe or hand work, the rows should be
14 to 16 inches apart. Spinach may be drilled
by hand in furrows about 1 inch deep and covered with fine earth not more than ½ inch deep,
or it may be drilled with a seed drill, which
distributes the seed more evenly than is ordinarily possible by hand. Thin the plants to 3
or 4 inches apart before they crowd in the row.

New Zealand Spinach

New Zealand spinach is not related to common spinach. It is a large plant, with thick, succulent leaves and stems, and grows with a
branching, spreading habit to a height of 2 or
more feet. It thrives in hot weather and is
grown as a substitute in seasons when ordinary
spinach cannot withstand the heat. New Zealand spinach thrives on soils suitable for common spinach. Because of their larger size, these

plants must have more room. The rows should be at least 3 feet apart, with the plants about 1½ feet apart in the rows. As prompt germination may be difficult, the seeds should be soaked for 1 or 2 hours in water at 120° F. before being planted. They may be sown, 1 to 1½ inches deep, as soon as danger of frost is past. Successive harvests of the tips may be made from a single planting, as new leaves and branches are readily produced. Care must be taken not to remove too large a portion of the plant at one time.

Turnip Greens

Varieties of turnips usually grown for the roots are also planted for the greens. Shogoin is a favorable variety for greens. It is resistant to aphid damage and produces fine-quality white roots if allowed to grow. Seven Top is a leafy sort that produces no edible root. As a rule, sow turnips to be used for greens thickly and then thin them, leaving all but the greens to develop as a root crop. Turnip greens are especially adapted to winter and early-spring culture in the South. The cultural methods employed are the same as those for turnip and rutabaga.

Salad Vegetables

The group known as salad crops includes vegetables that are usually eaten raw with salt, pepper, vinegar, and salad oil, or with mayonnaise or other dressings. This classification is entirely one of convenience; some vegetables not included in this group are used in the same way. Some members of this class may be cooked and used as greens.

Celery

Celery can be grown in home gardens in most parts of the country at some time during the year. It is a cool-weather crop and adapted to winter culture in the lower South. In the upper South and in the North it may be grown either as an early-spring or as a late-fall crop. Farther north in certain favored locations it can be grown throughout the summer.

Rich, moist but well-drained, deeply prepared, mellow soil is essential for celery. Soil varying from sand to clay loam and to peat may be used as long as these requirements are met. Unless the ground is very fertile, plenty of organic material, supplemented by liberal applications of commercial fertilizer, is necessary. For a 100-foot row of celery, 5 pounds of a high-grade complete fertilizer thoroughly mixed with the soil are none too much. Prepare the celery row a week or two before setting the plants.

The most common mistake with celery is failure to allow enough time for growing the plants. About 10 weeks are needed to grow good celery plants. Celery seed is small and germinates slowly. A good method is to place the seeds in a muslin bag and soak them overnight, then mix them with dry sand, distribute them in shallow trenches in the seed flats or seedbed, and cover them with leafmold or similar material to a depth of not more than ½ inch. Keep the bed covered with moist burlap sacks. Celery plants are very delicate and must be kept free from weeds. They are made more stocky by being transplanted once before they are set in the garden, but this practice retards their growth. When they are to be transplanted before being set in the ground, the rows in the seed box or seedbed may be only a few inches apart. When they are to remain in the box until transplanted to the garden, however, the plants should be about 2 inches apart each way. In beds, the rows should be 10 to 12 inches apart, with seedlings 1 to 1½ inches apart in the row.

For hand culture celery plants are set in rows 18 to 24 inches apart; for tractor cultivation 30 to 36 inches apart. The plants are spaced about 6 inches in the row. Double rows are about a foot apart. Set celery on a cool or cloudy day, if possible; and if the soil is at all dry, water the plants thoroughly. If the plants are large, it is best to pinch off the outer leaves 3 or 4 inches from the base before setting. In bright weather it is well also to shade the plants for a day or two after they are set. Small branches bearing green leaves, stuck in the ground, protect the plants from intense sun without excluding air. As soon as the plants attain some size, gradually work the soil around them to keep them upright. Be careful to get no soil into the hearts of the plants. Early celery is blanched by excluding the light with boards, paper, drain tiles, or other devices. Late celery may be blanched also by banking with earth or by storing in the dark. Banking celery with soil in warm weather causes it to decay.

Late celery may be kept for early-winter use by banking with earth and covering the tops with leaves or straw to keep them from freezing, or it may be dug and stored in a cellar or a coldframe, with the roots well embedded in moist soil. While in storage it must be kept as cool as possible without freezing.

For the home garden Golden Detroit, Summer Pascal (Waltham Improved), and the Golden Plume are adapted for the early crop to be used during late summer, fall, and early winter. For storage and for use after the holiday season, it is desirable to plant some such variety as Green Light or Utah 52–70.

Endive

Endive closely resembles lettuce in its requirements, except that it is less sensitive to heat. It may be substituted for lettuce when the culture of lettuce is impracticable. In the South, it is mainly a winter crop. In the North, it is grown in spring, summer, and autumn and is also forced in winter. Full Heart Batavian and Salad King are good varieties. Broadleaved endive is known on the markets as escarole.

Cultural details are the same as those for head lettuce. When the plants are large and well-formed, draw the leaves together and tie them so that the heart will blanch. For winter use, lift the plants with a ball of earth, place them in a cellar or coldframe where they will not freeze, and tie and blanch them as needed.

Lettuce

Lettuce can be grown in any home garden. It is a cool-weather crop, being as sensitive to heat as any vegetable grown. In the South, lettuce culture is confined to late fall, winter, and spring. In colder parts of the South, lettuce may not live through the winter. In the North, lettuce culture is particially limited to spring and autumn. In some favored locations, such as areas of high altitude or in far-northern latitudes, lettuce grows to perfection in summer.

Planting at a wrong season is responsible for most of the failures with this crop.

Any rich soil is adapted to lettuce, although the plant is sensitive to acid soil. A commercial fertilizer with a heavy proportion of phosphorus is recommended.

Start spring lettuce indoors or in a hotbed and transplant it to the garden when the plants have four of five leaves. Gardeners need not wait for the end of light frosts, as lettuce is not usually harmed by a temperature as low as 28° F., if the plants have been properly hardened. Allow about 6 weeks for growing the plants. For the fall crop the seed may be sown directly in the row and thinned; there is no gain in transplanting.

For tractor cultivation, set lettuce plants 12 to 15 inches apart in rows 30 to 36 inches apart; for hand culture, about 14 to 16 inches apart each way. Where gardeners grow leaf lettuce or desire merely the leaves and not well-developed heads, the spacing in the rows may be much closer. In any case it is usually best to cut the entire plant instead of removing the leaves.

There are many excellent varieties of lettuce, all of which do well in the garden when conditions are right. Of the loose-leaf kinds, Black-Seeded Simpson, Grand Rapids, Slobolt, and Saladbowl (fig. 18) are among the best. Saladbowl and Slobolt are heat resistant and very desirable for warm-weather culture. Of the heading sorts, Buttercrunch, White Boston, Fulton, and Great Lakes are among the best. The White Boston requires less time than the three others. Where warm weather comes early, it is seldom worth while to sow head lettuce seed in the open ground in the spring with the expectation of obtaining firm heads.

PN–2627

Figure 18.—Saladbowl lettuce is an outstanding leaf lettuce with considerable heat resistance.

Parsley

Parsley is hardy to cold but sensitive to heat. It thrives under much the same temperature conditions as kale, lettuce, and spinach. If given a little protection it may be carried over winter through most of the North.

Parsley thrives on any good soil. As the plant is delicate during its early stages of growth, however, the land should be mellow.

Parsley seeds are small and germinate slowly. Soaking in water overnight hastens the germination. In the North, it is a good plan to sow the seeds indoors and transplant the plants to the garden, thereby getting a crop before hot weather. In the South, it is usually possible to sow the seed directly in drills. For the fall crop in the North, row seeding is also practiced. After seeding, it is well to lay a board over the row for a few days until the first seedlings appear. After its removal day-to-day watering will insure germination of as many seeds as possible. Parsley rows should be 14 to 16 inches apart, with the plants 4 to 6 inches apart in the rows. A few feet will supply the family, and a few plants transplanted to the coldframe in the autumn will give a supply during early spring.

Upland Cress

Upland cress, sometimes erroneously called peppergrass, is a hardy plant. It may be sown in all the milder parts of the country in autumn. In the colder sections it is sown in early spring as soon as the ground can be worked. The seeds are small and must not be covered deeply. After the plants are well established, thin them to 4 to 6 inches apart in the rows. This is a short-season crop that should be planted in quick succession to insure a steady supply.

Root Vegetables

Potatoes in the North and sweetpotatoes in the South are grown in almost every garden. Beets, carrots, and turnips are also widely grown in gardens. The vegetables in this group may be used throughout the growing season and also be kept for winter.

Beet

The beet is well adapted to all parts of the country. It is fairly tolerant of heat; it is also resistant to cold. However, it will not withstand severe freezing. In the Northern States, where winters are too severe, the beet is grown in spring, summer, and autumn.

Beets are sensitive to strongly acid soils, and it is wise to apply lime if a test shows the need for it. Good beet quality depends on quick growth; for this the land must be fertile, well-drained, and in good physical condition.

Midsummer heat and drought may interfere with seed germination. By covering the seeds with sandy soil, leafmold, or other material that will not bake and by keeping the soil damp until the plants are up, much of this trouble can be avoided. Make successive sowings at intervals of about 3 weeks in order to have a continuous supply of young, tender beets throughout the season.

Where cultivating is by hand, the rows may be about 16 inches apart; where it is by tractor, they must be wider. Beet seed as purchased consists of small balls, each containing several seeds. On most soils the seed should be covered to a depth of about an inch. After the plants are well established, thin them to stand 2 to 3 inches apart in the rows.

Early Wonder, Crosby Egyptian, and Detroit Dark Red are standard varieties suitable for early home-garden planting, while Long Season remains tender and edible over a long season.

Carrot

Carrots are usually grown in the fall, winter, and spring in the South, providing an almost continuous supply. In the North, carrots can be grown and used through the summer and the surplus stored for winter. Carrots will grow on almost any type of soil as long as it is moist, fertile, loose, and free from clods and stones, but sandy loams and peats are best. Use commercial fertilizer.

Because of their hardiness, carrots may be seeded as early in the spring as the ground can be worked. Succession plantings at intervals of 3 weeks will insure a continuous supply of tender carrots. Cover carrot seed about ½ inch on most soils; less, usually about ¼ inch, on heavy soils. With care in seeding, little thinning is necessary; carrots can stand some crowding, especially on loose soils. However, they should be no thicker than 10 to 15 plants per foot of row.

Chantenay, Nantes, and Imperator are standard sorts. Carrots should be stored before hard frosts occur, as the roots may be injured by cold.

Celeriac

Celeriac, or turnip-rooted celery, has been developed for the root instead of the top. Its culture is the same as that of celery, and the enlarged roots can be used at any time after they are big enough. The late-summer crop of celeriac may be stored for winter use. In areas having mild winters the roots may be left in the ground and covered with a mulch of several inches of straw or leaves, or they may be lifted, packed in moist sand, and stored in a cool cellar.

Chervil

Chervil comes in two distinct types, salad chervil and turnip-rooted chervil. Salad chervil is grown about like parsley. The seeds must be bedded in damp sand for a few weeks before being sown; otherwise, their germination is very slow.

Turnip-rooted chervil thrives in practically all parts of the country where the soil is fertile and the moisture sufficient. In the South, the seeds are usually sown in the fall, but they may not germinate until spring. In the North, the seeds may be sown in the autumn to germinate in the spring; or the plants may be started indoors in later winter and transplanted to open ground later on. The spacing and culture of chervil are about the same as for beets and carrots.

Dasheen

The dasheen, a large-growing plant, is related to the ordinary elephant's-ear and looks like it. It is a long-season crop, adapted for culture only in the South, where there is normally a very warm frostless season of at least 7 months. It needs a rich loamy soil, an abundance of moisture with good drainage, and a fairly moist atmosphere. Small tubers—from 2 to 5 ounces in weight—are used for planting in much the same way as potatoes. Planting may be done 2 or 3 weeks before frosts are over, and the season may be lengthened by starting the plants indoors and setting them out after frost is past. Set the plants in 3½- to 4-foot

rows, about 2 feet apart in the rows. Dasheen
tubers may be dug and dried on the ground in
much the same way as sweetpotatoes, and
stored at 50° F. with ventilation.

Parsnip

The parsnip is adapted to culture over a wide
portion of the United States. It must have
warm soil and weather at planting time, but
does not thrive in midsummer in the South.

In many parts of the South parsnips are
grown and used during early summer. They
should not reach maturity during midsummer,
however. Furthermore, it is difficult to obtain
good germination in the summer, which limits
their culture during the autumn.

Any deep, fertile soil will grow parsnips, but
light, friable soil, with no tendency to bake, is
best. Stony or lumpy soils are objectionable;
they may cause rough, prongy roots.

Parsnip seed must be fresh—not more than a
year old–and it is well to sow rather thickly
and thin to about 3 inches apart. Parsnips germinate slowly, but it is possible to hasten germination by covering the seed with leafmold,
sand, a mixture of sifted coal ashes and soil,
peat, or some similar material that will not
bake. Rolling a light soil over the row or
trampling it firmly after seeding usually
hastens and improves germination. Hollow
Crown and All American are suitable varieties.

Parsnips may be dug and stored in a cellar or
pit or left in the ground until used. Roots
placed in cold storage gain in quality faster
than those left in the ground, and freezing in
the ground in winter improves the quality.

There is no basis for the belief that parsnips that remain in the ground over winter and start growth in the spring are poisonous. All reported cases of poisoning from eating so-called wild parsnips have been traced to water hemlock (*Cicuta*), which belongs to the same family and resembles the parsnip somewhat.

Be very careful in gathering wild plants that look like the parsnip.

Potato

Potatoes, when grown under favorable conditions, are one of the most productive of all vegetables in terms of food per unit area of land.

Potatoes are a cool-season crop; they do not thrive in midsummer in the southern half of the country. Any mellow, fertile, well-drained soil is suitable for potato production. Stiff, heavy clay soils often produce misshapen tubers. Potatoes respond to a generous use of commercial fertilizer, but if the soil is too heavily limed, the tubers may be scabby.

Commercial 5–8–5 or 5–8–7 mixtures applied at 1,000 to 2,000 pounds to the acre (approximately 7½ to 15 pounds to each 100-foot row) usually provide enough plant food for a heavy crop. The lower rate of application is sufficient for very fertile soils; the higher rate for less fertile ones. Commercial fertilizer can be applied at the time of planting, but it should be mixed with the soil in such a way that the seed pieces will not come in direct contact with it.

In the North, plant two types of potatoes— one to provide early potatoes for summer use, the other for storage and winter use. Early varieties include Irish Cobbler, Early Gem, Norland, Norgold Russet, and Superior. Best late varieties are Katahdin, Kennebec, Chippewa, Russet Burbank, Sebago, and the golden nemotode resistant Wanseon. Irish Cobbler is the most widely adapted of the early varieties and Katahdin of the late. In the Great Plains States, Pontiac and Red La Soda are preferred for summer use; the Katahdin and Russet Burbank for winter. In the Pacific Northwest, the Russet Burbank, White Rose, Kennebec, and Early Gem are used. In the Southern States, the Irish Cobbler, Red La Soda, Red Pontiac, and Pungo are widely grown. The use of certified seed is always advisable.

In preparing seed potatoes for planting, cut them into blocky rather than wedge-shaped pieces. Each piece should be about 1½ ounces in weight and have at least one eye. Medium-sized tubers weighing 5 to 7 ounces are cut to best advantage.

Plant early potatoes as soon as weather and soil conditions permit. Fall preparation of the soil often makes it possible to plant the early crop without delay in late winter or early spring. Potatoes require 2 to 3 weeks to come up, depending on depth of planting and the temperature of the soil. In some sections the ground may freeze slightly, but this is seldom harmful unless the sprouts have emerged. Prolonged cold and wet weather after planting is likely to cause the seed pieces to rot. Hence, avoid too early planting. Young potato plants are often damaged by frost, but they usually renew their growth quickly from uninjured portions of the stems.

Do not dig potatoes intended for storage until the tops are mature. Careful handling to avoid skinning is desirable, and protection from long exposure to light is necessary to prevent their becoming green and unfit for table use. Store in a well-ventilated place where the temperature is low, 45° to 50° if possible, but where there is no danger of freezing.

Radish

Radishes are hardy to cold, but they cannot withstand heat. In the South, they do well in autumn, winter, and spring. In the North, they may be grown in spring and autumn, and in sections having mild winters they may be grown in coldframes at that season. In high altitudes and in northern locations with cool summers, radishes thrive from early spring to late autumn.

Radishes are not sensitive to the type of soil so long as it is rich, moist, and friable. Apply additional fertilizer when the seeds are sown; conditions must be favorable for quick growth. Radishes that grow slowly have a pungent flavor and are undesirable.

Radishes mature the quickest of our garden crops. They remain in prime condition only a few days, which makes small plantings at week or 10-day intervals advisable. A few yards of row will supply all the radishes a family will consume during the time the radishes are at their best.

There are two types of radishes—the mild, small, quick-maturing sorts such as Scarlet

Globe, French Breakfast, and Cherry Belle, all
of which reach edible size in from 20 to 40
days; and the more pungent, large, winter
radishes such as Long Black Spanish and China
Rose, which require 75 days or more for
growth. Plant winter radishes so they will
reach a desirable size in the autumn. Gather
and store them like other root crops.

Salsify

Salsify, or vegetable oyster, may be grown
in practically all parts of the country. It is
similar to parsnips in its requirements but
needs a slightly longer growing season. For
this reason it cannot be grown as far north as
parsnips. Salsify, however, is somewhat more
hardy and can be sown earlier in the spring.

Thoroughly prepare soil for salsify to a
depth of at least a foot. Lighten heavy garden
soil by adding sand or comparable material.
Salsify must have plenty of plant food.

Sandwich Island is the best-known variety.
A half ounce of seed will sow a 50-foot row,
enough for most families. Always use fresh
seed; salsify seed retains its vitality only 1
year.

Salsify may be left in the ground over winter
or lifted and stored like parsnips or other root
crops.

Sweetpotato

Sweetpotatoes succeed best in the South, but
they are grown in home gardens as far north as
southern New York and southern Michigan.
They can be grown even farther north, in sections having especially mild climates, such as

the Pacific Northwest. In general, sweet-potatoes may be grown wherever there is a frost-free period of about 150 days with relatively high temperature. Jersey Orange, Nugget, and Nemagold are the commonest dry-fleshed varieties; Centennial, Porto Rico, and Goldrush are three of the best of the moist type.

A well-drained, moderately deep sandy loam of medium fertility is best for sweetpotatoes. Heavy clays and very deep loose-textured soils encourage the formation of long stringy roots. For best results the soil should be moderately fertilized throughout. If applied under the rows, the fertilizer should be well mixed with the soil.

In most of the area over which sweetpotatoes are grown it is necessary to start the plants in a hotbed, because the season is too short to produce a good crop after the weather warms enough to start plants outdoors. Bed roots used for seed close together in a hotbed and cover them with about 2 inches of sand or fine soil, such as leafmold. It is not safe to set the plants in the open ground until the soil is warm and the weather settled. Toward the last, ventilate the hotbed freely to harden the plants.

The plants are usually set on top of ridges, 3½ to 4 feet apart, with the plants about 12 inches apart in the row. When the vines have covered the ground, no further cultivation is necessary, but some additional hand weeding may be required.

Dig sweetpotatoes a short time before frost, on a bright, drying day when the soil is not too wet to work easily. On a small scale they may be dug with a spading fork, great care being taken not to bruise or injure the roots. Let the roots lie exposed for 2 or 3 hours to dry thoroughly; then put them in containers and place them in a warm room to cure. The proper curing temperature is 85° F. Curing for about 10 days is followed by storage at 50° to 55°.

Turnip and Rutabaga

Turnips and rutabagas, similar cool-season vegetables, are among the most commonly grown and widely adapted root crops in the United States. They are grown in the South chiefly in the fall, winter, and spring; in the North, largely in the spring and autumn. Rutabagas do best in the more northerly areas; turnips are better for gardens south of the latitude of Indianapolis, Ind., or northern Virginia.

Turnips reach a good size in from 60 to 80 days, but rutabagas need about a month longer. Being susceptible to heat and hardy to cold, these crops should be planted as late as possible for fall use, allowing time for maturity before hard frost. In the South, turnips are very popular in the winter and spring. In the North, however, July to August seeding, following early potatoes, peas, or spinach, is the common practice.

Land that has been in a heavily fertilized crop, such as early potatoes, usually gives a good crop without additional fertilizing. The soil need not be prepared deeply, but the surface should be fine and smooth. For spring culture, row planting similar to that described for beets is the best practice. The importance of planting turnips as early as possible for the spring crop is emphasized. When seeding in rows, cover the seeds lightly; when broadcasting, rake the seeds in lightly with a garden rake. A half ounce of seed will sow a 300-foot row or broadcast 300 square feet. Turnips may be thinned as they grow, and the tops used for greens.

Although there are both white-fleshed and yellow-fleshed varieties of turnips and rutabagas, most turnips are white-fleshed and most rutabagas are yellow-fleshed. Purple Top White Globe and Just Right are the most popular white-fleshed varieties; Golden Ball (Orange Jelly) is the most popular yellow-fleshed variety. American Purple Top is the commonly grown yellow-fleshed rutabaga; Sweet German (White Swede, Sweet Russian) is the most widely used white-fleshed variety. For turnip greens, the Seven Top variety is most suitable. This winter-hardy variety overwinters in a majority of locations in the United States.

Turnip-Rooted Parsley

The root is the edible portion of turnip-rooted parsley. The flesh is whitish and dry, with much the same flavor as celeriac.

Turnip-rooted parsley requires the same climate, soil, and culture as parsley. It can withstand much cold, but is difficult to start in dry, hot weather. This vegetable may remain in the ground until after hard frosts. It may be lifted and stored like other root crops.

Vine Vegetables

The vine crops, including cucumbers, muskmelons, pumpkins, squashes, watermelons, and citrons, are similar in their cultural requirements. In importance to the home gardener they do not compare with some other groups, especially the root crops and the greens, but there is a place in most gardens for at least bush squashes and a few hills of cucumbers. They all make rank growth and require much space. In large gardens, muskmelons and watermelons are often desirable.

Cucumber

Cucumbers are a warm-weather crop. They may be grown during the warmer months over a wide portion of the country, but are not adapted to winter growing in any but a few of the most southerly locations. Moreover, the extreme heat of midsummer in some places is too severe, and there cucumber culture is limited to spring and autumn.

The cucumber demands an exceedingly fertile, mellow soil high in decomposed organic matter from the compost pile. Also, an additional application of organic matter and commercial fertilizer is advisable under the rows or hills. Be sure the organic matter contains no remains of any vine crops; they might carry injurious diseases. Three or four wheelbarrow loads of well-rotted organic matter and 5 pounds of commercial fertilizer to a 50-foot drill or each 10 hills are enough. Mix the organic matter and fertilizer well with the top 8 to 10 inches of soil.

For an early crop, the seed may be started in berry boxes or pots, or on sods in a hotbed, and moved to the garden after danger of late frost is past. During the early growth and in cool periods, cucumbers may be covered with plant protectors made of panes of glass with a top of cheesecloth, parchment paper, or muslin. A few hills will supply the needs of a family.

When the seed is planted in drills, the rows should be 6 or 7 feet apart, with the plants thinned to 2 to 3 feet apart in the rows. In the hill method of planting, the hills should be at least 6 feet apart each way, with the plants thinned to 2 in each hill. It is always wise to plant 8 or 10 seeds in each hill, thinned to the desired stand. Cover the seeds to a depth of about ½ inch. If the soil is inclined to bake, cover them with loose earth, such as a mixture of soil and coarse sand, or other material that will not harden and keep the plants from coming through.

When cucumbers are grown primarily for pickling, plant one of the special small-size pickling varieties, such as Chicago Pickling or National Pickling; if they are grown for slicing, plant such varieties as White Spine or Straight Eight. It is usually desirable to plant a few hills of each type; both types can be used for either purpose.

Cucumbers require almost constant vigilance to prevent destructive attacks by cucumber beetles. These insects not only eat the foliage but also spread cucumber wilt and other serious diseases.

Success in growing cucumbers depends largely on the control of diseases and insect pests that attack the crop.

Removal of the fruits before any hard seeds form materially lengthens the life of the plants and increases the size of the crop.

Gourd

Gourds have the same general habit of growth as pumpkins and squashes and should have the same general cultural treatment, except that most species require some form of support or trellis to climb upon.

Gourds are used in making dippers, spoons, ladles, salt and sugar containers, and many

PN–2628

Figure 19.—An assorted collection of ornamental gourds.

other kinds of household utensils. They are also used for birdhouses and the manufacture of calabash pipes. But they are of interest chiefly because of their ornamental and decorative possibilities (Fig. 19). The thin-shelled, or hard-drying, gourds are the most durable and are the ones that most commonly serve as decorations. The thick-fleshed gourds are more in the nature of pumpkins and squashes, and are almost as perishable.

The thin-shelled gourds of the Lagenaria group are gathered and cured at the time the shells begin to harden, the fruits become lighter in weight, and the tendrils on the vines near the gourds begin to shrivel and dry. For best results, give the gourds plenty of time to cure. Some kinds require 6 months or a year to cure.

The thick-shelled gourds of the Cucurbita group are more difficult to cure than the thin-shelled ones. Their beauty is of short duration; they usually begin to fade after 3 or 4 months.

All types of gourds should be handled carefully. Bruises discolor them and cause them to soften and decay.

Muskmelon

The climatic, soil, and cultural requirements of muskmelons are about the same as for cucumbers, except that they are less tolerant of high humidity and rainy weather. They develop most perfectly on light-textured soils. The plants are vigorous growers, and need a somewhat wider spacing than cucumbers.

Hearts of Gold, Hale's Best, and Rocky Ford, the last-named a type not a variety, are usually grown in the home garden. Where powdery mildew is prevalent, resistant varieties such as Gulf Stream, Dulce, and Perlita are better adapted. Osage and Pride of Wisconsin (Queen of Colorado) are desirable home-garden sorts, particularly in the Northern States. Sweet Air (Knight) is a popular sort in the Maryland-Virginia area.

The Casaba and Honey Dew are well adapted only to the West, where they are grown under irrigation.

Pumpkin

Pumpkins are sensitive to both cold and heat. In the North, they cannot be planted until settled weather; in the South they do not thrive during midsummer.

The gardener is seldom jusified in devoting any part of a limited garden area to pumpkins, because many other vegetables give greater returns from the same space. However, in gardens where there is plenty of room and where they can follow an early crop like potatoes, pumpkins can often be grown to advantage.

The pumpkin is one of the few vegetables that thrives under partial shade. Therefore it may be grown among sweet corn or other tall plants. Small Sugar and Connecticut Field are well-known orange-yellow-skinned varieties. The Kentucky Field has a grayish-orange rind with salmon flesh. All are good-quality, productive varieties.

Hills of pumpkins, containing one to two plants, should be at least 10 feet apart each way. Pumpkin plants among corn, potato, or other plants usually should be spaced 8 to 10 feet apart in every third or fourth row.

Gather and store pumpkins before they are injured by hard frosts. They keep best in a well-ventilated place where the temperature is a little above 50° F.

PN–2629
Figure 20.—A mulched plant of Yellow Straightneck summer squash.

Squash

Squashes are among the most commonly grown garden plants. They do well in practically all parts of the United States where the soil is fertile and moisture sufficient. Although sensitive to frost, squashes are more hardy than melons and cucumbers. In the warmest parts of the South they may be grown in winter. The use of well-rotted composted material thoroughly mixed with the soil is recommended.

There are two classes of squash varieties, summer and winter. The summer class includes the Bush Scallop, known in some places as the Cymling, the Summer Crookneck, Straightneck, and Zucchini. It also includes the vegetable marrows, of which the best known sort is Italian Vegetable Marrow (Cocozelle). All the summer squashes and the marrows must be used while young and tender, when the rind can be easily penetrated by the thumbnail. The winter squashes include varieties such as Hubbard, Delicious, Table Queen (Acorn), and Boston Marrow. They have hard rinds and are well adapted for storage.

Summer varieties, like yellow Straightneck (fig. 20), should be gathered before the seeds ripen or the rinds harden, but the winter sorts will not keep unless well-matured. They should be taken in before hard frosts and stored in a dry, moderately warm place, such as on shelves in a basement with a furnace. Under favorable conditions such varieties as Hubbard may be kept until midwinter.

Watermelon

Only gardeners with a great deal of space can afford to grow watermelons. Moreover, they are rather particular in their soil requirements, a sand or sandy loam being best. Watermelon hills should be at least 8 feet apart. The plan of mixing a half wheelbarrow load of composted material with the soil in each hill is good, provided the compost is free from the remains of cucurbit plants that might carry diseases. A half pound of commercial fertilizer also should be thoroughly mixed with the soil in the hill. It is a good plan to place several seeds in a ring about 1 foot in diameter in each hill. Later the plants should be thinned to two to each hill.

New Hampshire Midget, Rhode Island Red, and Charleston Gray are suitable varieties for the home garden. New Hampshire Midget and Sugar Baby are small, extra early, widely grown, very productive varieties. The oval fruits are about 5 inches in diameter; they have crisp, red flesh and dark seeds. Rhode Island Red is an early variety. The fruits are medium in size, striped, and oval; they have a firm rind and bright pink-red flesh of choice quality. Charleston Gray is a large, long, high-quality, gray-green watermelon with excellent keeping and shipping qualities. It is resistant to anthracnose and fusarium wilt and requires a long growing season.

The preserving type of watermelon—citron —is not edible when raw. Its culture is the same as that for watermelon.

Legumes

Beans and peas are among our oldest and most important garden plants. The popularity of both is enhanced by their wide climatic and soil adaptation.

Beans

Green beans, both snap and lima, are more important than dry beans to the home gardener.

Snap beans cannot be planted until the ground is thoroughly warm, but succession plantings may be made every 2 weeks from that time until 7 or 8 weeks before frost. In the lower South and Southwest, green beans may be grown during the fall, winter, and spring, but they are not well adapted to midsummer. In the extreme South, beans are grown throughout the winter.

Green beans are adapted to a wide range of soils as long as the soils are well drained, reasonably fertile, and of such physical nature that they do not interfere with germination and emergence of the plants. Soil that has received a general application of manure and fertilizer should need no additional fertilization. When beans follow early crops that have been fertilized, the residue of this fertilizer is often sufficient for the beans.

On very heavy lands it is well to cover the planted row with sand, a mixture of sifted coal ashes and sand, peat, leafmold, or other material that will not bake. Bean seed should be covered not more than 1 inch in heavy soils and $1\frac{1}{2}$ inches in sandy soils. When beans are planted in hills, they may be covered with plant protectors. These covers make it possible to plant somewhat earlier.

Tendercrop (fig. 21), Topcrop, Tenderette, Contender, Harvester, and Kinghorn Wax are good bush varieties of snap beans. Dwarf Horticultural is an outstanding green-shell bean. Brown-seeded or white-seeded Kentucky Wonders are the best pole varieties for snap pods. White Navy, or pea beans, white or red Kidney, and the horticultural types are excellent for dry-shell purposes.

Two types of lima beans, called butter beans in the South, are grown in home gardens. Most of the more northerly parts of the United States, including the northern New England

PN–2630
Figure 21.—Tendercrop is a mosaic-resistant, heavy yielding snap bean with tender, round, green pods and a wide range of adaptability.

States and the northern parts of other States along the Canadian border, are not adapted to the culture of lima beans. Lima beans need a growing season of about 4 months with relatively high temperature; they cannot be planted safely until somewhat later than snap beans. The small butter beans mature in a shorter period than the large-seeded lima beans. The use of plant protectors over the seeds is an aid in obtaining earliness.

Lima beans may be grown on almost any fertile, well-drained, mellow soil, but it is especially desirable that the soil be light-textured and not subject to baking, as the seedlings cannot force their way through a hard crust. Covering with some material that will not bake, as suggested for other beans, is a wise precaution when using heavy soils. Lima beans need a soil somewhat richer than is necessary for kidney beans, but the excessive use of fertilizer containing a high percentage of nitrogen should be avoided.

Both the small- and large-seeded lima beans are available in pole and bush varieties. In the South, the most commonly grown lima bean varieties are Jackson Wonder, Nemagreen, Henderson Bush, and Sieva pole; in the North, Thorogreen, Dixie Butterpea, and Thaxter are popular small-seeded bush varieties. Fordhook 242 (fig. 22) is the most popular midseason large, thick-seeded bush lima bean. King of the Garden and Challenger are the most popular large-seeded pole lima bean varieties.

Pole beans of the kidney and lima types require some form of support, as they normally make vines several feet long. A 5-foot fence makes the best support for pole beans. A more complicated support can be prepared from 8-foot metal fence posts, spaced about 4 feet apart and connected horizontally and diagonally with coarse stout twine to make a trellis. Bean plants usually require some assistance to get started on these supports. Never cultivate

PN–2631

Figure 22.—Fordhook 242 bush lima beans are vigorous, productive, and heat-resistant.

or handle bean plants when they are wet; to do so is likely to spread disease.

English Peas

English peas are a cool-weather crop and should be planted early. In the lower South they are grown at all seasons except summer; farther north, in spring and autumn. In the

Northern States and at high altitudes, they may be grown from spring until autumn, although in many places summer heat is too severe and the season is practically limited to spring. A few succession plantings may be made at 10-day intervals. The later plantings rarely yield as well as the earlier ones. Planting may be resumed as the cool weather of autumn approaches, but the yield is seldom as satisfactory as that from the spring planting.

Alaska and other smooth-seeded varieties are frequently used for planting in the early spring because of the supposition that they can germinate well in cold, wet soil. Thomas Laxton, Greater Progress, Little Marvel, Freezonia, and Giant Stride are recommended as suitable early varieties with wrinkled seeds. Wando has considerable heat resistance. Alderman and Lincoln are approximately 2 weeks later than Greater Progress, but under favorable conditions yield heavily. Alderman is a desirable variety for growing on brush or a trellis. Peas grown on supports are less liable to destruction by birds.

Sugar Peas

Sugar peas (edible podded peas) possess the tenderness and fleshy podded qualities of snap beans and the flavor and sweetness of fresh English peas. When young, the pods are cooked like snap beans; the peas are not shelled. At this stage, pods are stringless, brittle, succulent, and free of fiber or parchment. However, if the pods develop too fast, they are not good to use like snap beans, but the seeds may be eaten as shelled peas and are of the best flavor before they have reached full size. Dwarf Gray Sugar is the earliest and dwarfest sugar pea. It is ideal for home gardens, especially where space is limited and seasons are short. A larger and later variety, Mammoth Melting Sugar, is resistant to fusarium wilt and requires support to climb upon.

Blackeye Peas

Blackeye peas, also known as cowpeas or Southern table peas, are highly nutritious, tasty, and easily grown. Do not plant until danger of frost has passed because they are very susceptible to cold. Leading varieties are Dixilee, Brown Crowder, Lady, Conch, White Acre, Louisiana Purchase, Texas Purple Hull 49, Knuckle Purple Hull, and Monarch Blackeye. Dixilee is a later variety of southern pea. Quality is excellent and it yields considerably more than such old standbys as blackeyes and crowders. It is also quite resistant, or at least tolerant, to nematodes. This fact alone makes it a desirable variety wherever this pest is present. Monarch Blackeye is a fairly new variety of the blackeye type and much better adapted to southern conditions.

Heavy applications of nitrogen fertilizer should not be used for southern peas. Fertilize moderately with a low-nitrogen analysis such as 4–12–12.

For the effort necessary to grow them, few if any other vegetables will pay higher dividends than Southern table peas.

Soybeans

The soil and cultural requirements and

methods of growing soybeans are essentially the
same as for bush forms of common beans. Soybeans, however, are slower growing than most
garden beans, requiring 3 to 5 months for maturity, and warmer weather. They also are
taller growing, the larger, later varieties requiring a greater distance between rows than
dwarf snap beans. Small, early varieties may
be planted in rows as close as 2 feet, but the
larger, later ones require 3 feet between rows.
The planting dates given in tables 4 and 5 are
for midseason varieties (about 120 days),
neither the earliest nor the latest kinds. Differences in time of development among varieties
are so great that the gardener must choose the
proper variety and know its time of maturity
in making plans for planting in any particular
locality. Kanrich and Giant Green are the most
widely grown varieties.

In cooler sections the rate of development will
be slower. Only the early varieties should be
grown in the more northerly States, and the
medium or late varieties in the South. Plantings
should be made principally when tomatoes and
other long-season, warm-weather crops are put
in the garden.

For use as a green vegetable, soybean pods
should be harvested when the seeds are fully
grown but before the pods turn yellow. Most
varieties produce beans in usable condition
over a period of a week to 10 days. The green
beans are difficult to remove from the pods unless the pods are boiled or steamed 4 to 5
minutes, after which they are easily shelled.

The yields per unit area of land are about the
same as are usually obtained with peas and are

thus less than can be obtained with many other vegetables. On this account, they appear of major interest only to gardeners having medium to large gardens.

Cabbage Group

The cabbage, or cole, group of vegetables is noteworthy because of its adaptation to culture in most parts of the country having fertile soil and sufficient moisture and because of its hardiness to cold.

Broccoli

Heading broccoli is difficult to grow, therefore, only sprouting broccoli is discussed here. Sprouting broccoli forms a loose flower head (on a tall, green, fleshy, branching stalk) instead of a compact head or curd found on cauliflower or heading broccoli. It is one of the newer vegetables in American gardens, but has been grown by Europeans for hundreds of years.

Sprouting broccoli is adapted to winter culture in areas suitable for winter cabbage. It is also tolerant of heat. Spring-set plants in the latitude of Washington, D.C., have yielded good crops of sprouts until midsummer and later under conditions that caused cauliflower to fail. In the latitude of Norfolk, Va., the plant has yielded good crops of sprouts from December until spring.

Sprouting broccoli is grown in the same way as cabbage. Plants grown indoors in the early spring and set in the open about April 1 begin to yield sprouts about 10 weeks later. The fall crop may be handled in the same way as late cabbage, except that the seed is sown later. The sprouts carrying flower buds are cut about 6 inches long, and other sprouts arise in the axils of the leaves, so that a continuous harvest may be obtained (fig. 23). Green Comet, Calabrese, and Waltham 29 are among the best known varieties.

PN–2632

Figure 23.—Sprouting broccoli with center head and side shoots.

Brussels Sprouts

Brussels sprouts are somewhat more hardy than cabbage and will live outdoors over winter in all the milder sections of the country. They may be grown as a winter crop in the South and as early and late as cabbage in the North. The sprouts, or small heads, are formed in the axils (the angle between the leaf stem and the main stalk) of the leaves. As the heads begin to crowd, break the lower leaves from the stem of the plant to give them more room. Always leave the top leaves; the plant needs them to supply nourishment. For winter use in cold areas, take up the plants that are well laden with heads and set them close together in a pit, a cold-frame, or a cellar, with some soil tamped around the roots. Keep the stored plants as cool as possible without freezing. Jade Cross, a true F_1 hybrid, has a wide range of adaptability.

Cabbage

Cabbage ranks as one of the most important home-garden crops. In the lower South, it can be grown in all seasons except summer, and in latitudes as far north as Washington, D.C., it is frequently set in the autumn, as its extreme hardiness enables it to live over winter at relatively low temperatures and thus become one of the first spring garden crops. Farther north, it can be grown as an early summer crop and as a late fall crop for storage. Cabbage can be grown throughout practically the entire United States.

Cabbage is adapted to widely different soils as long as they are fertile, of good texture, and moist. It is a heavy feeder; no vegetable responds better to favorable growing conditions. Quality in cabbage is closely associated with quick growth. Both compost and commercial fertilizer should be liberally used. In addition to the applications made at planting time, a side dressing or two of nitrate of soda, sulfate of ammonia, or other quickly available nitrogenous fertilizer is advisable. These may be applied sparingly to the soil around the plants at intervals of 3 weeks, not more than 1 pound being used to each 200 square feet of space, or, in terms of single plants, 1/3 ounce to each plant. For late cabbage the supplemental feeding with nitrates may be omitted. Good seed is especially important. Only a few seed is needed for starting enough plants for the home garden, as 2 or 3 dozen heads of early cabbage are as many as the average family can use. Early Jersey Wakefield and Golden Acre are standard early sorts. Copenhagen Market and Globe are excellent midseason kinds. Flat Dutch and Danish Ballhead are largely used for late planting.

Where cabbage yellows is a serious disease, resistant varieties should be used. The following are a few of the wilt-resistant varieties adapted to different seasons: Wisconsin Hollander, for late storage; Wisconsin All Seasons, a kraut cabbage, somewhat earlier; Marion Market and Globe, round-head cabbages, for midseason; and Stonehead for an early, small, round-head variety.

Cabbage plants for spring setting in the North may be grown in hotbeds or greenhouses from seeding made a month to 6 weeks before planting time, or may be purchased from southern growers who produce them outdoors in winter. The winter-grown, hardened plants, sometimes referred to as frostproof, are hardier than hotbed plants and may be set outdoors in most parts of the North as soon as the ground can be worked in the spring. Northern gardeners can have cabbage from their gardens much earlier by using healthy southern-grown plants or well-hardened, well-grown hotbed or greenhouse plants. Late cabbage, prized by northern gardeners for fall use and for storage, is grown from plants produced in open seedbeds from sowings made about a month ahead of planting. Late cabbage may well follow early potatoes, peas, beets, spinach, or other early crop. Many gardeners set cabbage plants between potato rows before the potatoes are ready to dig, thereby gaining time. In protected places, or when plant protectors are used, it is possible always to advance dates somewhat, especially if the plants are well hardened.

Chinese Cabbage

Chinese cabbage, (fig. 24) is more closely related to mustard than to cabbage. It is variously called Crispy Choy, Chihili, Michili, and Wong Bok. Also, it is popularly known as celery cabbage, although it is unrelated to celery. The nonheading types deserve greater attention.

Chinese cabbage seems to do best as an autumn crop in the northern tier of States. When fullgrown, it is an attractive vegetable. It is not especially successful as a spring crop, and gardeners are advised not to try to grow it at any season other than fall in the North or in winter in the South.

The plant demands a very rich, well-drained but moist soil. The seeds may be sown and the plants transplanted to the garden, or the seed may be drilled in the garden rows and the plants thinned to the desired stand.

PN–2633

Figure 24.—Chinese cabbage is a desirable autumn crop in the Northern States.

Cauliflower

Cauliflower (fig. 25) is a hardy vegetable but it will not withstand as much frost as cabbage. Too much warm weather keeps cauliflower from heading. In the South, its culture is limited to fall, winter, and spring; in the North, to spring and fall. However, in some areas of high altitude and when conditions are otherwise favorable, cauliflower culture is continuous throughout the summer.

Cauliflower is grown on all types of land from sands to clay and peats. Although the physical character is unimportant, the land must be fertile and well drained. Manure and commercial fertilizer are essential.

The time required for growing cauliflower plants is the same as for cabbage. In the North, the main cause of failure with cauliflower in the spring is delay in sowing the seed and setting the plants. The fall crop must be planted at such a time that it will come to the heading stage in cool weather. Snowball and Purple Head are standard varieties of cauliflower. Snow King is an extremely early variety with

Figure 25.—A good head of cauliflower on a plant mulched with hay.

fair sized, compact heads of good quality; it has very short stems. Always take care to obtain a good strain of seed; poor cauliflower seed is most objectionable. The Purple Head variety, well adapted for the home garden, turns green when cooked.

A necessary precaution in cauliflower culture with all varieties, except Purple Head, is to tie the leaves together when the heads, or buttons, begin to form. This keeps the heads white. Cauliflower does not keep long after the heads form; 1 or 2 dozen heads are enough for the average garden in one season.

Kohlrabi

Kohlrabi is grown for its swollen stem. In the North, the early crop may be started like cabbage and transplanted to the garden, but usually it is sown in place. In the South, kohlrabi may be grown almost any time except midsummer. The seeds may be started indoors and the plants transplanted in the garden; or the seeds may be drilled in the garden rows and the plants thinned to the desired stand. Kohlrabi has about the same soil and cultural requirements as cabbage, principally a fertile soil and enough moisture. It should be harvested while young and tender. Standard varieties are Purple Vienna and White Vienna.

Onion Group

Practically all members of the onion group are adapted to a wide variety of soils. Some of them can be grown at one time of the year or another in any part of the country that has fertile soil and ample moisture. They require but little garden space to produce enough for a family's needs.

PN–2635

Figure 26.—A pot of chives grown in a kitchen window.

Chives

Chives are small onionlike plants (fig. 26) that will grow in any place where onions do well. They are frequently planted as a border, but are equally well adapted to culture in rows. Being a perennial, chives should be planted where they can be left for more than one season.

Chives may be started from either seed or clumps of bulbs. Once established, some of the bulbs can be lifted and moved to a new spot. When left in the same place for several years the plants become too thick; occasionally dividing and resetting is desirable.

Garlic

Garlic is more exacting in its cultural requirements than are onions, but it may be grown with a fair degree of success in almost any home garden where good results are obtained with onions.

Garlic is propagated by planting the small cloves, or bulbs, which make up the large bulbs. Each large bulb contains about 10 small ones. Carefully separate the small bulbs and plant them singly.

The culture of garlic is practically the same as tnat of onions. When mature the bulbs are pulled, dried, and braided into strings or tied in bunches, which are hung in a cool, well-ventilated place.

In the South, where the crop matures early, care must be taken to keep the garlic in a cool, dry place; otherwise it spoils. In the North, where the crop matures later in the season, storage is not so difficult, but care must be taken to prevent freezing.

Leek

The leek resembles the onion in its adaptability and cultural requirements. Instead of forming a bulb it produces a thick, fleshy cylinder like a large green onion (fig. 27). Leeks are started from seeds, like onions. Usually the seeds are sown in a shallow trench, so that the plants can be more easily hilled up as growth proceeds. Leeks are ready for use any time after they reach the right size. Under favorable conditions they grow to 1½ inches or more in diameter, with white parts 6 to 8 inches long. They may be lifted in the autumn and stored like celery in a coldframe or a cellar.

PN–2636

Figure 27.—Leeks are used for almost any purpose that onions are used for.

Onion

Onions thrive under a wide variety of climatic and soil conditions, but do best with an abundance of moisture and a temperate climate, without extremes of heat or cold through the growing season. In the South, the onion thrives in the fall, winter, and spring. Farther north, winter temperatures may be too severe for certain types. In the North, onions are primarily a spring, summer, and fall crop.

Any type of soil will grow onions, but it must be fertile, moist, and in the highest state of tilth. Both compost and commercial fertilizer, especially one high in phosphorus and potash, should be applied to the onion plot. A pound of compost to each square foot of ground and 4 or 5 pounds of fertilizer to each 100 square feet are about right. The soil should be very fine and free from clods and foreign matter.

Onions may be started in the home garden by the use of sets, seedlings, or seed. Sets, or small dry onions grown the previous year—preferably not more than ¾ inch in diameter—are usually employed by home gardeners. Small green plants grown in an outdoor seedbed in the South or in a hotbed or a greenhouse are also in general use. The home-garden culture of onions from seed is satisfactory in the North where the summers are comparatively cool.

Sets and seedlings cost about the same; seeds cost much less. In certainty of results the seedlings are best; practically none form seedstalks. Seed-sown onions are uncertain unless conditions are extremely favorable.

Several distinct types of onions may be grown. The Potato (Multiplier) and Top (Tree) onions are planted in the fall or early spring for use green. Yellow Bermuda, Granex, and White Granex are large, very mild, flat onions for spring harvest in the South; they have short storage life. Sweet Spanish and the hybrids Golden Beauty, Fiesta, Bronze, Perfection, El Capitan are large, mild, globular onions suited for growing in the middle latitudes of the country; they store moderately well. Southport White Globe, Southport Yellow

Globe, Ebenezer, Early Yellow Globe, Yellow Globe Danvers, and the hybrid Abundance are all firm-fleshed, long-storage onions for growing as a "main crop" in the Northeast and Midwest. Early Harvest is an early F_1 hybrid adapted to all northern regions of the United States. Varieties that produce bulbs may also be used green.

Shallot

The shallot is a small onion of the Multiplier type. Its bulbs have a more delicate flavor than most onions. Its growth requirements are about the same as those of most other onions. Shallots seldom form seed and are propagated by means of the small cloves or divisions, into which the plant splits during growth. The plant is hardy and may be left in the ground from year to year, but best results are had by lifting the clusters of bulbs at the end of the growing season and replanting the smaller ones at the desired time.

Fleshy-Fruited Vegetables

The fleshy-fruited, warm-season vegetables, of which the tomato is the most important, are closely related and have about the same cultural requirements. All must have warm weather and fertile, well-drained soil for good results.

Eggplant

Eggplant is extremely sensitive to the conditions under which it is grown. A warm-weather plant, it demands a growing season of from 100 to 140 days with high average day and night temperatures. The soil, also, must be well warmed up before eggplant can safely be set outdoors.

In the South, eggplants are grown in spring and autumn; in the North, only in summer. The more northerly areas, where a short growing season and low summer temperatures pre-

PN–2637

Figure 28.—The eggplant is a popular vegetable that requires little space.

vail, are generally unsuitable for eggplants. In very fertile garden soil, which is best for eggplant, a few plants will yield a large number of fruits.

Sow eggplant seeds in a hotbed or greenhouse, or, in warm areas, outdoors about 8 weeks before the plants are to be transplanted. It is important that the plants be kept growing without check from low or drying temperatures or other causes. They may be transplanted like tomatoes. Good plants have stems that are not hard or woody; one with a woody stem rarely develops satisfactorily. Black Beauty (fig. 28), Early Beauty Hybrid, and Jersey King Hybrid are good varieties.

Pepper

Peppers are more exacting than tomatoes in their requirements, but may be grown over a wide range in the United States. Being hot-weather plants, peppers cannot be planted in

PN–2638

Figure 29.—California Wonder variety of pepper.

the North until the soil has warmed up and all danger of frost is over. In the South, planting dates vary with the location, fall planting being practiced in some locations. Start pepper plants 6 to 8 weeks before needed. The seeds and plants require a somewhat higher temperature than those of the tomato. Otherwise they are handled in exactly the same way.

Hot peppers are represented by such varieties as Red Chili and Long Red Cayenne; the mild-flavored by Penn Wonder, Ruby King, World-beater, California Wonder (fig. 29), and Yale Wonder, which mature in the order given.

Tomato

Tomatoes grow under a wide variety of conditions and require only a relatively small space for a large production. Of tropical American origin, the tomato does not thrive in very cool weather. It will, however, grow in winter in home gardens in the extreme South. Over most of the upper South and the North, it is suited to spring, summer, and autumn culture. In the more northern areas, the growing season is likely to be too short for heavy yields, and it is often desirable to increase earliness and the length of the growing season by starting the plants indoors. By adopting a few precautions, the home gardener can grow tomatoes practically everywhere, given fertile soil with sufficient moisture.

A liberal application of compost and commercial fertilizer in preparing the soil should be sufficient for tomatoes under most conditions. Heavy applications of fertilizer should be broadcast, not applied in the row; but small quantities may be mixed with the soil in the row in preparing for planting.

Start early tomato plants from 5 to 7 weeks before they are to be transplanted to the garden. Enough plants for the home garden may be started in a window box and transplanted to small pots, paper drinking cups with the bottoms removed, plant bands (round or square), or other soil containers. In boxes, the

PN–2639

Figure 30.—Tomato plants staked with a wire cylinder to hold them off the ground so the fruit does not rot. The grass mulch around the plants controls weeds and conserves moisture.

seedlings are spaced 2 to 3 inches apart. Tomato seeds germinate best at about 70° F., or ordinary house temperature. Growing tomato seedlings, after the first transplanting, at moderate temperatures, with plenty of ventilation, as in a coldframe, gives stocky, hardy growth. If desired, the plants may be transplanted again to larger containers, such as 4-inch clay pots or quart cans with holes in the bottom.

Tomato plants for all but the early spring crop are usually grown in outdoor seedbeds. Thin seeding and careful weed control will give strong, stocky plants for transplanting. A list of tomato varieties for home garden use in areas other than the Southwest is given in table 6.

TABLE 6.—*Tomato varieties for areas other than the Southwest*

Variety	Area
Ace	West
Atkinson	South
C17	East, Midwest
Fireball VF	East, North
Floradel	South
R1350	East, Midwest
Homestead–24	South
Manalucie	South
Marion	South
Morton Hybrid	North, East
Moscow VR	West
Small Fry	All areas
Spring Giant	East, Midwest
Supermarket	South
Supersonic	East, Midwest
Tropi-Gro	South
VFW-8	West

In the Southwest, Pearson, Early Pack No. 7, VF 36, California 145, VF 13L, and Ace are grown.

Tomatoes are sensitive to cold. Never plant them until danger of frost is past. By using plant protectors during cool periods the home gardener can set tomato plants somewhat earlier than would otherwise be possible. Hot, dry weather, like mid-summer weather in the South is also unfavorable for planting tomatoes. Planting distances depend on the variety and on whether the plants are to be pruned and staked or not. If pruned to one stem, trained, and tied to stakes or a trellis, they may be set 18 inches apart in 3-foot rows (fig. 30) ; if not, they may be planted 3 feet apart in rows 4 to 5 feet apart. Pruning and staking have many advantages for the home gardener. Cultivation is easier, and the fruits are always clean and easy to find. Staked and pruned tomatoes are, however, more subject to losses from blossom-end rot than those allowed to grow naturally.

Miscellaneous Vegetables

Florence Fennel

Florence fennel is related to celery and celeriac. Its enlarged, flattened leafstalk is the portion used. For a summer crop, sow the seeds in the rows in spring; for an autumn and winter crop in the South, sow them toward the end of the summer. Thin the plants to stand about 6 inches apart. When the leafstalks have grown to about 2 inches in diameter the plants may be slightly mounded up and partially blanched. They should be harvested and used before they become tough and stringy.

Okra

Okra, or gumbo, has about the same degree of hardiness as cucumbers and tomatoes and may be grown under the same conditions. It thrives on any fertile, well-drained soil. An abundance of quickly available plant food will stimulate growth and insure a good yield of tender, high-quality pods.

As okra is a warm-weather vegetable, the seeds should not be sown until the soil is warm. The rows should be from 3 to 3½ feet apart, depending on whether the variety is dwarf or large growing. Sow the seeds every few inches and thin the plants to stand 18 inches to 2 feet apart in the rows. Clemson Spineless, Emerald, and Dwarf Green are good varieties. The pods should be picked young and tender, and none allowed to ripen. Old pods are unfit for use and soon exhaust the plant.

Physalis

Physalis known also as groundcherry and husk tomato, is closely related to the tomato and can be grown wherever tomatoes do well. The kind ordinarily grown in gardens produces a yellow fruit about the size of a cherry. The seeds may be started indoors or sown in rows in the garden.

Sweet Corn

Sweet corn requires plenty of space and is adapted only to the larger gardens. Although a warm-weather plant, it may be grown in practically all parts of the United States. It needs a fertile, well-drained, moist soil. With these requirements met, the type of the soil does not seem to be especially important, but a clay loam is almost ideal for sweet corn.

In the South, sweet corn is planted from early spring until autumn, but the corn earworm, drought, and heat make it difficult to obtain worthwhile results in midsummer. The ears pass the edible stage very quickly, and succession plantings are necessary to insure a constant supply. In the North, sweet corn cannot be safely planted until the ground has thoroughly warmed up. Here, too, succession plantings need to be made to insure a steady supply. Sweet corn is frequently planted to good advantage after early potatoes, peas, beets, lettuce, or other early, short-season crops. Sometimes, to gain time, it may be planted before the early crop is removed.

Sweet corn may be grown in either hills or drills, in rows at least 3 feet apart. It is well to plant the seed rather thickly and thin to single stalks 14 to 16 inches apart or three plants to each 3-foot hill. Experiments have shown that in the eastern part of the country there is no advantage in removing suckers from sweet corn. Cultivation sufficient to control weeds is all that is needed.

Hybrid sweet corn varieties, both white and yellow, are usually more productive than the open-pollinated sorts. As a rule, they need a more fertile soil and heavier feeding. They should be fertilized with 5–10–5 fertilizer about every 3 weeks until they start to silk. Many are resistant to disease, particularly bacterial wilt. Never save seed from a hybrid crop for planting. Such seed does not come true to the form of the plants from which it was harvested.

Good yellow-grained hybrids, in the order of the time required to reach edible maturity, are Span-cross, Marcross, Golden Beauty, Golden Cross Bantam, and Ioana. White-grained hybrids are Evergreen and Country Gentleman.

Well-known open-pollinated yellow sorts are Golden Bantam and Golden Midget. Open-pollinated white sorts, in the order of maturity, are Early Evergreen, Country Gentleman, and Stowell Evergreen.

STATE AGRICULTURAL EXPERIMENT STATIONS

ALABAMA
Auburn
ALASKA
College
ARIZONA
Tucson
ARKANSAS
Fayetteville
CALIFORNIA
Berkeley
Davis
Los Angeles
Riverside
Parlier
COLORADO
Fort Collins
CONNECTICUT
New Haven
Storrs
DELAWARE
Newark

FLORIDA
Gainesville
GEORGIA
Athens
Experiment
Tifton
HAWAII
Honolulu
IDAHO
Moscow
ILLINOIS
Urbana
INDIANA
LaFayette
IOWA
Ames
KANSAS
Manhattan
KENTUCKY
Lexington
LOUISIANA
Baton Rouge

MAINE
Orono
MARYLAND
College Park
MASSACHUSETTS
Amherst
MICHIGAN
East Lansing
MINNESOTA
St. Paul
MISSISSIPPI
State College
MISSOURI
Columbia
MONTANA
Bozeman
NEBRASKA
Lincoln
NEVADA
Reno
NEW HAMPSHIRE
Durham
NEW JERSEY
New Brunswick

NEW MEXICO
Las Cruces
NEW YORK
Geneva
Ithaca
NORTH CAROLINA
Raleigh
NORTH DAKOTA
Fargo
OHIO
Columbus
Wooster
OKLAHOMA
Stillwater
OREGON
Corvallis
PENNSYLVANIA
University Park
RHODE ISLAND
Kingston
SOUTH CAROLINA
Clemson

SOUTH DAKOTA
Brookings
TENNESSEE
Knoxville
TEXAS
College Station
UTAH
Logan
VERMONT
Burlington
VIRGINIA
Blacksburg
WASHINGTON
Pullman
WEST VIRGINIA
Morgantown
WISCONSIN
Madison
WYOMING
Laramie

INDEX OF VEGETABLES

Asparagus 56	Lettuce 71
Beans 93	Muskmelon 89
Beet 75	Mustard 66
Broccoli 101	Okra 119
Brussels sprouts 102	Onion 111
Cabbage 103	Parsley 73
Cabbage, Chinese 105	Parsley, turnip-rooted 85
Carrot 76	Parsnip 78
Cauliflower 106	Peas 97
Celeriac 76	Pepper 115
Celery 69	Physalis 120
Chard 62	Potato 79
Chervil 77	Pumpkin 90
Chicory, witloof 63	Radish 81
Chives 109	Rhubarb 60
Collards 64	Rutabaga 84
Cornsalad 64	Salsify 82
Corn, sweet 120	Shallot 113
Cress, upland 74	Sorrel 62
Cucumber 86	Soybeans 99
Dasheen 77	Spinach 66
Eggplant 113	Spinach, New Zealand 67
Endive 71	Squash 91
Fennel, Florence 119	Sweetpotato 82
Garlic 110	Tomato 116
Gourds 88	Turnip 84
Horseradish 59	Turnip greens 68
Kale 64	Watermelon 92
Kohlrabi 108	
Leek 110	

A CATALOGUE OF SELECTED DOVER BOOKS
IN ALL FIELDS OF INTEREST

A CATALOGUE OF SELECTED DOVER BOOKS
IN ALL FIELDS OF INTEREST

AMERICA'S OLD MASTERS, James T. Flexner. Four men emerged unexpectedly from provincial 18th century America to leadership in European art: Benjamin West, J. S. Copley, C. R. Peale, Gilbert Stuart. Brilliant coverage of lives and contributions. Revised, 1967 edition. 69 plates. 365pp. of text.
21806-6 Paperbound $3.00

FIRST FLOWERS OF OUR WILDERNESS: AMERICAN PAINTING, THE COLONIAL PERIOD, James T. Flexner. Painters, and regional painting traditions from earliest Colonial times up to the emergence of Copley, West and Peale Sr., Foster, Gustavus Hesselius, Feke, John Smibert and many anonymous painters in the primitive manner. Engaging presentation, with 162 illustrations. xxii + 368pp.
22180-6 Paperbound $3.50

THE LIGHT OF DISTANT SKIES: AMERICAN PAINTING, 1760-1835, James T. Flexner. The great generation of early American painters goes to Europe to learn and to teach: West, Copley, Gilbert Stuart and others. Allston, Trumbull, Morse; also contemporary American painters—primitives, derivatives, academics—who remained in America. 102 illustrations. xiii + 306pp.
22179-2 Paperbound $3.50

A HISTORY OF THE RISE AND PROGRESS OF THE ARTS OF DESIGN IN THE UNITED STATES, William Dunlap. Much the richest mine of information on early American painters, sculptors, architects, engravers, miniaturists, etc. The only source of information for scores of artists, the major primary source for many others. Unabridged reprint of rare original 1834 edition, with new introduction by James T. Flexner, and 394 new illustrations. Edited by Rita Weiss. 6⅝ x 9⅝.
21695-0, 21696-9, 21697-7 Three volumes, Paperbound $15.00

EPOCHS OF CHINESE AND JAPANESE ART, Ernest F. Fenollosa. From primitive Chinese art to the 20th century, thorough history, explanation of every important art period and form, including Japanese woodcuts; main stress on China and Japan, but Tibet, Korea also included. Still unexcelled for its detailed, rich coverage of cultural background, aesthetic elements, diffusion studies, particularly of the historical period. 2nd, 1913 edition. 242 illustrations. lii + 439pp. of text.
20364-6, 20365-4 Two volumes, Paperbound $6.00

THE GENTLE ART OF MAKING ENEMIES, James A. M. Whistler. Greatest wit of his day deflates Oscar Wilde, Ruskin, Swinburne; strikes back at inane critics, exhibitions, art journalism; aesthetics of impressionist revolution in most striking form. Highly readable classic by great painter. Reproduction of edition designed by Whistler. Introduction by Alfred Werner. xxxvi + 334pp.
21875-9 Paperbound $3.00

VISUAL ILLUSIONS: THEIR CAUSES, CHARACTERISTICS, AND APPLICATIONS, Matthew Luckiesh. Thorough description and discussion of optical illusion, geometric and perspective, particularly; size and shape distortions, illusions of color, of motion; natural illusions; use of illusion in art and magic, industry, etc. Most useful today with op art, also for classical art. Scores of effects illustrated. Introduction by William H. Ittleson. 100 illustrations. xxi + 252pp.
21530-X Paperbound $2.00

A HANDBOOK OF ANATOMY FOR ART STUDENTS, Arthur Thomson. Thorough, virtually exhaustive coverage of skeletal structure, musculature, etc. Full text, supplemented by anatomical diagrams and drawings and by photographs of undraped figures. Unique in its comparison of male and female forms, pointing out differences of contour, texture, form. 211 figures, 40 drawings, 86 photographs. xx + 459pp. 5⅜ x 8⅜.
21163-0 Paperbound $3.50

150 MASTERPIECES OF DRAWING, Selected by Anthony Toney. Full page reproductions of drawings from the early 16th to the end of the 18th century, all beautifully reproduced: Rembrandt, Michelangelo, Dürer, Fragonard, Urs, Graf, Wouwerman, many others. First-rate browsing book, model book for artists. xviii + 150pp. 8⅜ x 11¼.
21032-4 Paperbound' $3.50

THE LATER WORK OF AUBREY BEARDSLEY, Aubrey Beardsley. Exotic, erotic, ironic masterpieces in full maturity: Comedy Ballet, Venus and Tannhauser, Pierrot, Lysistrata, Rape of the Lock, Savoy material, Ali Baba, Volpone, etc. This material revolutionized the art world, and is still powerful, fresh, brilliant. With *The Early Work*, all Beardsley's finest work. 174 plates, 2 in color. xiv + 176pp. 8⅛ x 11.
21817-1 Paperbound $3.75

DRAWINGS OF REMBRANDT, Rembrandt van Rijn. Complete reproduction of fabulously rare edition by Lippmann and Hofstede de Groot, completely reedited, updated, improved by Prof. Seymour Slive, Fogg Museum. Portraits, Biblical sketches, landscapes, Oriental types, nudes, episodes from classical mythology—All Rembrandt's fertile genius. Also selection of drawings by his pupils and followers. "Stunning volumes," *Saturday Review*. 550 illustrations. lxxviii + 552pp. 9⅛ x 12¼.
21485-0, 21486-9 Two volumes, Paperbound $10.00

THE DISASTERS OF WAR, Francisco Goya. One of the masterpieces of Western civilization—83 etchings that record Goya's shattering, bitter reaction to the Napoleonic war that swept through Spain after the insurrection of 1808 and to war in general. Reprint of the first edition, with three additional plates from Boston's Museum of Fine Arts. All plates facsimile size. Introduction by Philip Hofer, Fogg Museum. v + 97pp. 9⅜ x 8¼.
21872-4 Paperbound $2.50

GRAPHIC WORKS OF ODILON REDON. Largest collection of Redon's graphic works ever assembled: 172 lithographs, 28 etchings and engravings, 9 drawings. These include some of his most famous works. All the plates from *Odilon Redon: oeuvre graphique complet,* plus additional plates. New introduction and caption translations by Alfred Werner. 209 illustrations. xxvii + 209pp. 9⅛ x 12¼.
21966-8 Paperbound $5.00

DESIGN BY ACCIDENT; A BOOK OF "ACCIDENTAL EFFECTS" FOR ARTISTS AND DESIGNERS, James F. O'Brien. Create your own unique, striking, imaginative effects by "controlled accident" interaction of materials: paints and lacquers, oil and water based paints, splatter, crackling materials, shatter, similar items. Everything you do will be different; first book on this limitless art, so useful to both fine artist and commercial artist. Full instructions. 192 plates showing "accidents," 8 in color. viii + 215pp. 8⅜ x 11¼. 21942-9 Paperbound $3.75

THE BOOK OF SIGNS, Rudolf Koch. Famed German type designer draws 493 beautiful symbols: religious, mystical, alchemical, imperial, property marks, runes, etc. Remarkable fusion of traditional and modern. Good for suggestions of timelessness, smartness, modernity. Text. vi + 104pp. 6⅛ x 9¼.
20162-7 Paperbound $1.25

HISTORY OF INDIAN AND INDONESIAN ART, Ananda K. Coomaraswamy. An unabridged republication of one of the finest books by a great scholar in Eastern art. Rich in descriptive material, history, social backgrounds; Sunga reliefs, Rajput paintings, Gupta temples, Burmese frescoes, textiles, jewelry, sculpture, etc. 400 photos. viii + 423pp. 6⅜ x 9¾. 21436-2 Paperbound $5.00

PRIMITIVE ART, Franz Boas. America's foremost anthropologist surveys textiles, ceramics, woodcarving, basketry, metalwork, etc.; patterns, technology, creation of symbols, style origins. All areas of world, but very full on Northwest Coast Indians. More than 350 illustrations of baskets, boxes, totem poles, weapons, etc. 378 pp.
20025-6 Paperbound $3.00

THE GENTLEMAN AND CABINET MAKER'S DIRECTOR, Thomas Chippendale. Full reprint (third edition, 1762) of most influential furniture book of all time, by master cabinetmaker. 200 plates, illustrating chairs, sofas, mirrors, tables, cabinets, plus 24 photographs of surviving pieces. Biographical introduction by N. Bienenstock. vi + 249pp. 9⅞ x 12¾. 21601-2 Paperbound $4.00

AMERICAN ANTIQUE FURNITURE, Edgar G. Miller, Jr. The basic coverage of all American furniture before 1840. Individual chapters cover type of furniture—clocks, tables, sideboards, etc.—chronologically, with inexhaustible wealth of data. More than 2100 photographs, all identified, commented on. Essential to all early American collectors. Introduction by H. E. Keyes. vi + 1106pp. 7⅞ x 10¾.
21599-7, 21600-4 Two volumes, Paperbound $11.00

PENNSYLVANIA DUTCH AMERICAN FOLK ART, Henry J. Kauffman. 279 photos, 28 drawings of tulipware, Fraktur script, painted tinware, toys, flowered furniture, quilts, samplers, hex signs, house interiors, etc. Full descriptive text. Excellent for tourist, rewarding for designer, collector. Map. 146pp. 7⅞ x 10¾.
21205-X Paperbound $2.50

EARLY NEW ENGLAND GRAVESTONE RUBBINGS, Edmund V. Gillon, Jr. 43 photographs, 226 carefully reproduced rubbings show heavily symbolic, sometimes macabre early gravestones, up to early 19th century. Remarkable early American primitive art, occasionally strikingly beautiful; always powerful. Text. xxvi + 207pp. 8⅜ x 11¼. 21380-3 Paperbound $3.50

ALPHABETS AND ORNAMENTS, Ernst Lehner. Well-known pictorial source for decorative alphabets, script examples, cartouches, frames, decorative title pages, calligraphic initials, borders, similar material. 14th to 19th century, mostly European. Useful in almost any graphic arts designing, varied styles. 750 illustrations. 256pp. 7 x 10.   21905-4 Paperbound $4.00

PAINTING: A CREATIVE APPROACH, Norman Colquhoun. For the beginner simple guide provides an instructive approach to painting: major stumbling blocks for beginner; overcoming them, technical points; paints and pigments; oil painting; watercolor and other media and color. New section on "plastic" paints. Glossary. Formerly *Paint Your Own Pictures.* 221pp.   22000-1 Paperbound $1.75

THE ENJOYMENT AND USE OF COLOR, Walter Sargent. Explanation of the relations between colors themselves and between colors in nature and art, including hundreds of little-known facts about color values, intensities, effects of high and low illumination, complementary colors. Many practical hints for painters, references to great masters. 7 color plates, 29 illustrations. x + 274pp.
20944-X Paperbound $2.75

THE NOTEBOOKS OF LEONARDO DA VINCI, compiled and edited by Jean Paul Richter. 1566 extracts from original manuscripts reveal the full range of Leonardo's versatile genius: all his writings on painting, sculpture, architecture, anatomy, astronomy, geography, topography, physiology, mining, music, etc., in both Italian and English, with 186 plates of manuscript pages and more than 500 additional drawings. Includes studies for the Last Supper, the lost Sforza monument, and other works. Total of xlvii + 866pp. 7⅞ x 10¾.
22572-0, 22573-9 Two volumes, Paperbound $11.00

MONTGOMERY WARD CATALOGUE OF 1895. Tea gowns, yards of flannel and pillow-case lace, stereoscopes, books of gospel hymns, the New Improved Singer Sewing Machine, side saddles, milk skimmers, straight-edged razors, high-button shoes, spittoons, and on and on . . . listing some 25,000 items, practically all illustrated. Essential to the shoppers of the 1890's, it is our truest record of the spirit of the period. Unaltered reprint of Issue No. 57, Spring and Summer 1895. Introduction by Boris Emmet. Innumerable illustrations. xiii + 624pp. 8½ x 11⅝.
22377-9 Paperbound $6.95

THE CRYSTAL PALACE EXHIBITION ILLUSTRATED CATALOGUE (LONDON, 1851). One of the wonders of the modern world—the Crystal Palace Exhibition in which all the nations of the civilized world exhibited their achievements in the arts and sciences—presented in an equally important illustrated catalogue. More than 1700 items pictured with accompanying text—ceramics, textiles, cast-iron work, carpets, pianos, sleds, razors, wall-papers, billiard tables, beehives, silverware and hundreds of other artifacts—represent the focal point of Victorian culture in the Western World. Probably the largest collection of Victorian decorative art ever assembled— indispensable for antiquarians and designers. Unabridged republication of the Art-Journal Catalogue of the Great Exhibition of 1851, with all terminal essays. New introduction by John Gloag, F.S.A. xxxiv + 426pp. 9 x 12.
22503-8 Paperbound $5.00

A HISTORY OF COSTUME, Carl Köhler. Definitive history, based on surviving pieces of clothing primarily, and paintings, statues, etc. secondarily. Highly readable text, supplemented by 594 illustrations of costumes of the ancient Mediterranean peoples, Greece and Rome, the Teutonic prehistoric period; costumes of the Middle Ages, Renaissance, Baroque, 18th and 19th centuries. Clear, measured patterns are provided for many clothing articles. Approach is practical throughout. Enlarged by Emma von Sichart. 464pp.   21030-8 Paperbound $3.50.

ORIENTAL RUGS, ANTIQUE AND MODERN, Walter A. Hawley. A complete and authoritative treatise on the Oriental rug—where they are made, by whom and how, designs and symbols, characteristics in detail of the six major groups, how to distinguish them and how to buy them. Detailed technical data is provided on periods, weaves, warps, wefts, textures, sides, ends and knots, although no technical background is required for an understanding. 11 color plates, 80 halftones, 4 maps. vi + 320pp. 6⅛ x 9⅛.   22366-3 Paperbound $5.00

TEN BOOKS ON ARCHITECTURE, Vitruvius. By any standards the most important book on architecture ever written. Early Roman discussion of aesthetics of building, construction methods, orders, sites, and every other aspect of architecture has inspired, instructed architecture for about 2,000 years. Stands behind Palladio, Michelangelo, Bramante, Wren, countless others. Definitive Morris H. Morgan translation. 68 illustrations. xii + 331pp.   20645-9 Paperbound $3.00

THE FOUR BOOKS OF ARCHITECTURE, Andrea Palladio. Translated into every major Western European language in the two centuries following its publication in 1570, this has been one of the most influential books in the history of architecture. Complete reprint of the 1738 Isaac Ware edition. New introduction by Adolf Placzek, Columbia Univ. 216 plates. xxii + 110pp. of text. 9½ x 12¾.
                    21308-0 Clothbound $12.50

STICKS AND STONES: A STUDY OF AMERICAN ARCHITECTURE AND CIVILIZATION, Lewis Mumford.One of the great classics of American cultural history. American architecture from the medieval-inspired earliest forms to the early 20th century; evolution of structure and style, and reciprocal influences on environment. 21 photographic illustrations. 238pp.   20202-X Paperbound $2.00

THE AMERICAN BUILDER'S COMPANION, Asher Benjamin. The most widely used early 19th century architectural style and source book, for colonial up into Greek Revival periods. Extensive development of geometry of carpentering, construction of sashes, frames, doors, stairs; plans and elevations of domestic and other buildings. Hundreds of thousands of houses were built according to this book, now invaluable to historians, architects, restorers, etc. 1827 edition. 59 plates. 114pp. 7⅞ x 10¾.
                    22236-5 Paperbound $3.50

DUTCH HOUSES IN THE HUDSON VALLEY BEFORE 1776, Helen Wilkinson Reynolds. The standard survey of the Dutch colonial house and outbuildings, with constructional features, decoration, and local history associated with individual homesteads. Introduction by Franklin D. Roosevelt. Map. 150 illustrations. 469pp. 6⅝ x 9¼.   21469-9 Paperbound $5.00

THE ARCHITECTURE OF COUNTRY HOUSES, Andrew J. Downing. Together with Vaux's *Villas and Cottages* this is the basic book for Hudson River Gothic architecture of the middle Victorian period. Full, sound discussions of general aspects of housing, architecture, style, decoration, furnishing, together with scores of detailed house plans, illustrations of specific buildings, accompanied by full text. Perhaps the most influential single American architectural book. 1850 edition. Introduction by J. Stewart Johnson. 321 figures, 34 architectural designs. xvi + 560pp.
22003-6 Paperbound $4.00

LOST EXAMPLES OF COLONIAL ARCHITECTURE, John Mead Howells. Full-page photographs of buildings that have disappeared or been so altered as to be denatured, including many designed by major early American architects. 245 plates. xvii + 248pp. 7⅞ x 10¾. 21143-6 Paperbound $3.50

DOMESTIC ARCHITECTURE OF THE AMERICAN COLONIES AND OF THE EARLY REPUBLIC, Fiske Kimball. Foremost architect and restorer of Williamsburg and Monticello covers nearly 200 homes between 1620-1825. Architectural details, construction, style features, special fixtures, floor plans, etc. Generally considered finest work in its area. 219 illustrations of houses, doorways, windows, capital mantels. xx + 314pp. 7⅞ x 10¾. 21743-4 Paperbound $4.00

EARLY AMERICAN ROOMS: 1650-1858, edited by Russell Hawes Kettell. Tour of 12 rooms, each representative of a different era in American history and each furnished, decorated, designed and occupied in the style of the era. 72 plans and elevations, 8-page color section, etc., show fabrics, wall papers, arrangements, etc. Full descriptive text. xvii + 200pp. of text. 8⅜ x 11¼.
21633-0 Paperbound $5.00

THE FITZWILLIAM VIRGINAL BOOK, edited by J. Fuller Maitland and W. B. Squire. Full modern printing of famous early 17th-century ms. volume of 300 works by Morley, Byrd, Bull, Gibbons, etc. For piano or other modern keyboard instrument; easy to read format. xxxvi + 938pp. 8⅜ x 11.
21068-5, 21069-3 Two volumes, Paperbound $10.00

KEYBOARD MUSIC, Johann Sebastian Bach. Bach Gesellschaft edition. A rich selection of Bach's masterpieces for the harpsichord: the six English Suites, six French Suites, the six Partitas (Clavierübung part I), the Goldberg Variations (Clavierübung part IV), the fifteen Two-Part Inventions and the fifteen Three-Part Sinfonias. Clearly reproduced on large sheets with ample margins; eminently playable. vi + 312pp. 8⅛ x 11. 22360-4 Paperbound $5.00

THE MUSIC OF BACH: AN INTRODUCTION, Charles Sanford Terry. A fine, nontechnical introduction to Bach's music, both instrumental and vocal. Covers organ music, chamber music, passion music, other types. Analyzes themes, developments, innovations. x + 114pp. 21075-8 Paperbound $1.50

BEETHOVEN AND HIS NINE SYMPHONIES, Sir George Grove. Noted British musicologist provides best history, analysis, commentary on symphonies. Very thorough, rigorously accurate; necessary to both advanced student and amateur music lover. 436 musical passages. vii + 407 pp. 20334-4 Paperbound $2.75

JOHANN SEBASTIAN BACH, Philipp Spitta. One of the great classics of musicology, this definitive analysis of Bach's music (and life) has never been surpassed. Lucid, nontechnical analyses of hundreds of pieces (30 pages devoted to St. Matthew Passion, 26 to B Minor Mass). Also includes major analysis of 18th-century music. 450 musical examples. 40-page musical supplement. Total of xx + 1799pp.
(EUK) 22278-0, 22279-9 Two volumes, Clothbound $17.50

MOZART AND HIS PIANO CONCERTOS, Cuthbert Girdlestone. The only full-length study of an important area of Mozart's creativity. Provides detailed analyses of all 23 concertos, traces inspirational sources. 417 musical examples. Second edition. 509pp. 21271-8 Paperbound $3.50

THE PERFECT WAGNERITE: A COMMENTARY ON THE NIBLUNG'S RING, George Bernard Shaw. Brilliant and still relevant criticism in remarkable essays on Wagner's Ring cycle, Shaw's ideas on political and social ideology behind the plots, role of Leitmotifs, vocal requisites, etc. Prefaces. xxi + 136pp.
(USO) 21707-8 Paperbound $1.75

DON GIOVANNI, W. A. Mozart. Complete libretto, modern English translation; biographies of composer and librettist; accounts of early performances and critical reaction. Lavishly illustrated. All the material you need to understand and appreciate this great work. Dover Opera Guide and Libretto Series; translated and introduced by Ellen Bleiler. 92 illustrations. 209pp.
21134-7 Paperbound $2.00

BASIC ELECTRICITY, U. S. Bureau of Naval Personel. Originally a training course, best non-technical coverage of basic theory of electricity and its applications. Fundamental concepts, batteries, circuits, conductors and wiring techniques, AC and DC, inductance and capacitance, generators, motors, transformers, magnetic amplifiers, synchros, servomechanisms, etc. Also covers blue-prints, electrical diagrams, etc. Many questions, with answers. 349 illustrations. x + 448pp. 6½ x 9¼.
20973-3 Paperbound $3.50

REPRODUCTION OF SOUND, Edgar Villchur. Thorough coverage for laymen of high fidelity systems, reproducing systems in general, needles, amplifiers, preamps, loudspeakers, feedback, explaining physical background. "A rare talent for making technicalities vividly comprehensible," R. Darrell, *High Fidelity.* 69 figures. iv + 92pp. 21515-6 Paperbound $1.35

HEAR ME TALKIN' TO YA: THE STORY OF JAZZ AS TOLD BY THE MEN WHO MADE IT, Nat Shapiro and Nat Hentoff. Louis Armstrong, Fats Waller, Jo Jones, Clarence Williams, Billy Holiday, Duke Ellington, Jelly Roll Morton and dozens of other jazz greats tell how it was in Chicago's South Side, New Orleans, depression Harlem and the modern West Coast as jazz was born and grew. xvi + 429pp.
21726-4 Paperbound $3.00

FABLES OF AESOP, translated by Sir Roger L'Estrange. A reproduction of the very rare 1931 Paris edition; a selection of the most interesting fables, together with 50 imaginative drawings by Alexander Calder. v + 128pp. 6½x9¼.
21780-9 Paperbound $1.50

AGAINST THE GRAIN (A REBOURS), Joris K. Huysmans. Filled with weird images, evidences of a bizarre imagination, exotic experiments with hallucinatory drugs, rich tastes and smells and the diversions of its sybarite hero Duc Jean des Esseintes, this classic novel pushed 19th-century literary decadence to its limits. Full unabridged edition. Do not confuse this with abridged editions generally sold. Introduction by Havelock Ellis. xlix + 206pp.   22190-3 Paperbound $2.50

VARIORUM SHAKESPEARE: HAMLET. Edited by Horace H. Furness; a landmark of American scholarship. Exhaustive footnotes and appendices treat all doubtful words and phrases, as well as suggested critical emendations throughout the play's history. First volume contains editor's own text, collated with all Quartos and Folios. Second volume contains full first Quarto, translations of Shakespeare's sources (Belleforest, and Saxo Grammaticus), Der Bestrafte Brudermord, and many essays on critical and historical points of interest by major authorities of past and present. Includes details of staging and costuming over the years. By far the best edition available for serious students of Shakespeare. Total of xx + 905pp.
21004-9, 21005-7, 2 volumes, Paperbound $7.00

A LIFE OF WILLIAM SHAKESPEARE, Sir Sidney Lee. This is the standard life of Shakespeare, summarizing everything known about Shakespeare and his plays. Incredibly rich in material, broad in coverage, clear and judicious, it has served thousands as the best introduction to Shakespeare. 1931 edition. 9 plates. xxix + 792pp.   21967-4 Paperbound $4.50

MASTERS OF THE DRAMA, John Gassner. Most comprehensive history of the drama in print, covering every tradition from Greeks to modern Europe and America, including India, Far East, etc. Covers more than 800 dramatists, 2000 plays, with biographical material, plot summaries, theatre history, criticism, etc. "Best of its kind in English," New Republic. 77 illustrations. xxii + 890pp.
20100-7 Clothbound $10.00

THE EVOLUTION OF THE ENGLISH LANGUAGE, George McKnight. The growth of English, from the 14th century to the present. Unusual, non-technical account presents basic information in very interesting form: sound shifts, change in grammar and syntax, vocabulary growth, similar topics. Abundantly illustrated with quotations. Formerly Modern English in the Making. xii + 590pp.
21932-1 Paperbound $4.00

AN ETYMOLOGICAL DICTIONARY OF MODERN ENGLISH, Ernest Weekley. Fullest, richest work of its sort, by foremost British lexicographer. Detailed word histories, including many colloquial and archaic words; extensive quotations. Do not confuse this with the Concise Etymological Dictionary, which is much abridged. Total of xxvii + 830pp. 6½ x 9¼.
21873-2, 21874-0 Two volumes, Paperbound $7.90

FLATLAND: A ROMANCE OF MANY DIMENSIONS, E. A. Abbott. Classic of science-fiction explores ramifications of life in a two-dimensional world, and what happens when a three-dimensional being intrudes. Amusing reading, but also useful as introduction to thought about hyperspace. Introduction by Banesh Hoffmann. 16 illustrations. xx + 103pp.   20001-9 Paperbound $1.25

POEMS OF ANNE BRADSTREET, edited with an introduction by Robert Hutchinson. A new selection of poems by America's first poet and perhaps the first significant woman poet in the English language. 48 poems display her development in works of considerable variety—love poems, domestic poems, religious meditations, formal elegies, "quaternions," etc. Notes, bibliography. viii + 222pp.

22160-1 Paperbound $2.50

THREE GOTHIC NOVELS: THE CASTLE OF OTRANTO BY HORACE WALPOLE; VATHEK BY WILLIAM BECKFORD; THE VAMPYRE BY JOHN POLIDORI, WITH FRAGMENT OF A NOVEL BY LORD BYRON, edited by E. F. Bleiler. The first Gothic novel, by Walpole; the finest Oriental tale in English, by Beckford; powerful Romantic supernatural story in versions by Polidori and Byron. All extremely important in history of literature; all still exciting, packed with supernatural thrills, ghosts, haunted castles, magic, etc. xl + 291pp.

21232-7 Paperbound $2.50

THE BEST TALES OF HOFFMANN, E. T. A. Hoffmann. 10 of Hoffmann's most important stories, in modern re-editings of standard translations: Nutcracker and the King of Mice, Signor Formica, Automata, The Sandman, Rath Krespel, The Golden Flowerpot, Master Martin the Cooper, The Mines of Falun, The King's Betrothed, A New Year's Eve Adventure. 7 illustrations by Hoffmann. Edited by E. F. Bleiler. xxxix + 419pp. 21793-0 Paperbound $3.00

GHOST AND HORROR STORIES OF AMBROSE BIERCE, Ambrose Bierce. 23 strikingly modern stories of the horrors latent in the human mind: The Eyes of the Panther, The Damned Thing, An Occurrence at Owl Creek Bridge, An Inhabitant of Carcosa, etc., plus the dream-essay, Visions of the Night. Edited by E. F. Bleiler. xxii + 199pp. 20767-6 Paperbound $1.50

BEST GHOST STORIES OF J. S. LEFANU, J. Sheridan LeFanu. Finest stories by Victorian master often considered greatest supernatural writer of all. Carmilla, Green Tea, The Haunted Baronet, The Familiar, and 12 others. Most never before available in the U. S. A. Edited by E. F. Bleiler. 8 illustrations from Victorian publications. xvii + 467pp. 20415-4 Paperbound $3.00

MATHEMATICAL FOUNDATIONS OF INFORMATION THEORY, A. I. Khinchin. Comprehensive introduction to work of Shannon, McMillan, Feinstein and Khinchin, placing these investigations on a rigorous mathematical basis. Covers entropy concept in probability theory, uniqueness theorem, Shannon's inequality, ergodic sources, the E property, martingale concept, noise, Feinstein's fundamental lemma, Shanon's first and second theorems. Translated by R. A. Silverman and M. D. Friedman. iii + 120pp. 60434-9 Paperbound $2.00

SEVEN SCIENCE FICTION NOVELS, H. G. Wells. The standard collection of the great novels. Complete, unabridged. *First Men in the Moon, Island of Dr. Moreau, War of the Worlds, Food of the Gods, Invisible Man, Time Machine, In the Days of the Comet.* Not only science fiction fans, but every educated person owes it to himself to read these novels. 1015pp. (USO) 20264-X Clothbound $6.00

LAST AND FIRST MEN AND STAR MAKER, TWO SCIENCE FICTION NOVELS, Olaf Stapledon. Greatest future histories in science fiction. In the first, human intelligence is the "hero," through strange paths of evolution, interplanetary invasions, incredible technologies, near extinctions and reemergences. Star Maker describes the quest of a band of star rovers for intelligence itself, through time and space: weird inhuman civilizations, crustacean minds, symbiotic worlds, etc. Complete, unabridged. v + 438pp. (USO) 21962-3 Paperbound $2.50

THREE PROPHETIC NOVELS, H. G. WELLS. Stages of a consistently planned future for mankind. *When the Sleeper Wakes*, and *A Story of the Days to Come*, anticipate *Brave New World* and *1984*, in the 21st Century; *The Time Machine*, only complete version in print, shows farther future and the end of mankind. All show Wells's greatest gifts as storyteller and novelist. Edited by E. F. Bleiler. x + 335pp. (USO) 20605-X Paperbound $2.50

THE DEVIL'S DICTIONARY, Ambrose Bierce. America's own Oscar Wilde— Ambrose Bierce—offers his barbed iconoclastic wisdom in over 1,000 definitions hailed by H. L. Mencken as "some of the most gorgeous witticisms in the English language." 145pp. 20487-1 Paperbound $1.25

MAX AND MORITZ, Wilhelm Busch. Great children's classic, father of comic strip, of two bad boys, Max and Moritz. Also Ker and Plunk (Plisch und Plumm), Cat and Mouse, Deceitful Henry, Ice-Peter, The Boy and the Pipe, and five other pieces. Original German, with English translation. Edited by H. Arthur Klein; translations by various hands and H. Arthur Klein. vi + 216pp.
20181-3 Paperbound $2.00

PIGS IS PIGS AND OTHER FAVORITES, Ellis Parker Butler. The title story is one of the best humor short stories, as Mike Flannery obfuscates biology and English. Also included, That Pup of Murchison's, The Great American Pie Company, and Perkins of Portland. 14 illustrations. v + 109pp. 21532-6 Paperbound $1.25

THE PETERKIN PAPERS, Lucretia P. Hale. It takes genius to be as stupidly mad as the Peterkins, as they decide to become wise, celebrate the "Fourth," keep a cow, and otherwise strain the resources of the Lady from Philadelphia. Basic book of American humor. 153 illustrations. 219pp. 20794-3 Paperbound $2.00

PERRAULT'S FAIRY TALES, translated by A. E. Johnson and S. R. Littlewood, with 34 full-page illustrations by Gustave Doré. All the original Perrault stories— Cinderella, Sleeping Beauty, Bluebeard, Little Red Riding Hood, Puss in Boots, Tom Thumb, etc.—with their witty verse morals and the magnificent illustrations of Doré. One of the five or six great books of European fairy tales. viii + 117pp. 8⅛ x 11. 22311-6 Paperbound $2.00

OLD HUNGARIAN FAIRY TALES, Baroness Orczy. Favorites translated and adapted by author of the *Scarlet Pimpernel*. Eight fairy tales include "The Suitors of Princess Fire-Fly," "The Twin Hunchbacks," "Mr. Cuttlefish's Love Story," and "The Enchanted Cat." This little volume of magic and adventure will captivate children as it has for generations. 90 drawings by Montagu Barstow. 96pp.
(USO) 22293-4 Paperbound $1.95

THE RED FAIRY BOOK, Andrew Lang. Lang's color fairy books have long been children's favorites. This volume includes Rapunzel, Jack and the Bean-stalk and 35 other stories, familiar and unfamiliar. 4 plates, 93 illustrations x + 367pp.
21673-X Paperbound $2.50

THE BLUE FAIRY BOOK, Andrew Lang. Lang's tales come from all countries and all times. Here are 37 tales from Grimm, the Arabian Nights, Greek Mythology, and other fascinating sources. 8 plates, 130 illustrations. xi + 390pp.
21437-0 Paperbound $2.75

HOUSEHOLD STORIES BY THE BROTHERS GRIMM. Classic English-language edition of the well-known tales — Rumpelstiltskin, Snow White, Hansel and Gretel, The Twelve Brothers, Faithful John, Rapunzel, Tom Thumb (52 stories in all). Translated into simple, straightforward English by Lucy Crane. Ornamented with head-pieces, vignettes, elaborate decorative initials and a dozen full-page illustrations by Walter Crane. x + 269pp.
21080-4 Paperbound **$2.00**

THE MERRY ADVENTURES OF ROBIN HOOD, Howard Pyle. The finest modern versions of the traditional ballads and tales about the great English outlaw. Howard Pyle's complete prose version, with every word, every illustration of the first edition. Do not confuse this facsimile of the original (1883) with modern editions that change text or illustrations. 23 plates plus many page decorations. xxii + 296pp.
22043-5 Paperbound $2.75

THE STORY OF KING ARTHUR AND HIS KNIGHTS, Howard Pyle. The finest children's version of the life of King Arthur; brilliantly retold by Pyle, with 48 of his most imaginative illustrations. xviii + 313pp. 6⅛ x 9¼.
21445-1 Paperbound $2.50

THE WONDERFUL WIZARD OF OZ, L. Frank Baum. America's finest children's book in facsimile of first edition with all Denslow illustrations in full color. The edition a child should have. Introduction by Martin Gardner. 23 color plates, scores of drawings. iv + 267pp.
20691-2 Paperbound $2.50

THE MARVELOUS LAND OF OZ, L. Frank Baum. The second Oz book, every bit as imaginative as the Wizard. The hero is a boy named Tip, but the Scarecrow and the Tin Woodman are back, as is the Oz magic. 16 color plates, 120 drawings by John R. Neill. 287pp.
20692-0 Paperbound $2.50

THE MAGICAL MONARCH OF MO, L. Frank Baum. Remarkable adventures in a land even stranger than Oz. The best of Baum's books not in the Oz series. 15 color plates and dozens of drawings by Frank Verbeck. xviii + 237pp.
21892-9 Paperbound $2.25

THE BAD CHILD'S BOOK OF BEASTS, MORE BEASTS FOR WORSE CHILDREN, A MORAL ALPHABET, Hilaire Belloc. Three complete humor classics in one volume. Be kind to the frog, and do not call him names . . . and 28 other whimsical animals. Familiar favorites and some not so well known. Illustrated by Basil Blackwell. 156pp.
(USO) 20749-8 Paperbound $1.50

EAST O' THE SUN AND WEST O' THE MOON, George W. Dasent. Considered the best of all translations of these Norwegian folk tales, this collection has been enjoyed by generations of children (and folklorists too). Includes True and Untrue, Why the Sea is Salt, East O' the Sun and West O' the Moon, Why the Bear is Stumpy-Tailed, Boots and the Troll, The Cock and the Hen, Rich Peter the Pedlar, and 52 more. The only edition with all 59 tales. 77 illustrations by Erik Werenskiold and Theodor Kittelsen. xv + 418pp. 22521-6 Paperbound $3.50

GOOPS AND HOW TO BE THEM, Gelett Burgess. Classic of tongue-in-cheek humor, masquerading as etiquette book. 87 verses, twice as many cartoons, show mischievous Goops as they demonstrate to children virtues of table manners, neatness, courtesy, etc. Favorite for generations. viii + 88pp. 6½ x 9¼.
22233-0 Paperbound $1.50

ALICE'S ADVENTURES UNDER GROUND, Lewis Carroll. The first version, quite different from the final Alice in Wonderland, printed out by Carroll himself with his own illustrations. Complete facsimile of the "million dollar" manuscript Carroll gave to Alice Liddell in 1864. Introduction by Martin Gardner. viii + 96pp. Title and dedication pages in color. 21482-6 Paperbound $1.25

THE BROWNIES, THEIR BOOK, Palmer Cox. Small as mice, cunning as foxes, exuberant and full of mischief, the Brownies go to the zoo, toy shop, seashore, circus, etc., in 24 verse adventures and 266 illustrations. Long a favorite, since their first appearance in St. Nicholas Magazine. xi + 144pp. 6⅝ x 9¼.
21265-3 Paperbound $1.75

SONGS OF CHILDHOOD, Walter De La Mare. Published (under the pseudonym Walter Ramal) when De La Mare was only 29, this charming collection has long been a favorite children's book. A facsimile of the first edition in paper, the 47 poems capture the simplicity of the nursery rhyme and the ballad, including such lyrics as I Met Eve, Tartary, The Silver Penny. vii + 106pp. (USO) 21972-0 Paperbound $2.00

THE COMPLETE NONSENSE OF EDWARD LEAR, Edward Lear. The finest 19th-century humorist-cartoonist in full: all nonsense limericks, zany alphabets, Owl and Pussycat, songs, nonsense botany, and more than 500 illustrations by Lear himself. Edited by Holbrook Jackson. xxix + 287pp. (USO) 20167-8 Paperbound $2.00

BILLY WHISKERS: THE AUTOBIOGRAPHY OF A GOAT, Frances Trego Montgomery. A favorite of children since the early 20th century, here are the escapades of that rambunctious, irresistible and mischievous goat—Billy Whiskers. Much in the spirit of Peck's Bad Boy, this is a book that children never tire of reading or hearing. All the original familiar illustrations by W. H. Fry are included: 6 color plates, 18 black and white drawings. 159pp. 22345-0 Paperbound $2.00

MOTHER GOOSE MELODIES. Faithful republication of the fabulously rare Munroe and Francis "copyright 1833" Boston edition—the most important Mother Goose collection, usually referred to as the "original." Familiar rhymes plus many rare ones, with wonderful old woodcut illustrations. Edited by E. F. Bleiler. 128pp. 4½ x 6⅜. 22577-1 Paperbound $1.00

Two Little Savages; Being the Adventures of Two Boys Who Lived as Indians and What They Learned, Ernest Thompson Seton. Great classic of nature and boyhood provides a vast range of woodlore in most palatable form, a genuinely entertaining story. Two farm boys build a teepee in woods and live in it for a month, working out Indian solutions to living problems, star lore, birds and animals, plants, etc. 293 illustrations. vii + 286pp.

20985-7 Paperbound $2.50

Peter Piper's Practical Principles of Plain & Perfect Pronunciation. Alliterative jingles and tongue-twisters of surprising charm, that made their first appearance in America about 1830. Republished in full with the spirited woodcut illustrations from this earliest American edition. 32pp. $4\frac{1}{2}$ x $6\frac{3}{8}$.

22560-7 Paperbound $1.00

Science Experiments and Amusements for Children, Charles Vivian. 73 easy experiments, requiring only materials found at home or easily available, such as candles, coins, steel wool, etc.; illustrate basic phenomena like vacuum, simple chemical reaction, etc. All safe. Modern, well-planned. Formerly *Science Games for Children*. 102 photos, numerous drawings. 96pp. $6\frac{1}{8}$ x $9\frac{1}{4}$.

21856-2 Paperbound $1.25

An Introduction to Chess Moves and Tactics Simply Explained, Leonard Barden. Informal intermediate introduction, quite strong in explaining reasons for moves. Covers basic material, tactics, important openings, traps, positional play in middle game, end game. Attempts to isolate patterns and recurrent configurations. Formerly *Chess*. 58 figures. 102pp.   (USO) 21210-6 Paperbound $1.25

Lasker's Manual of Chess, Dr. Emanuel Lasker. Lasker was not only one of the five great World Champions, he was also one of the ablest expositors, theorists, and analysts. In many ways, his Manual, permeated with his philosophy of battle, filled with keen insights, is one of the greatest works ever written on chess. Filled with analyzed games by the great players. A single-volume library that will profit almost any chess player, beginner or master. 308 diagrams. xli x 349pp.

20640-8 Paperbound $2.75

The Master Book of Mathematical Recreations, Fred Schuh. In opinion of many the finest work ever prepared on mathematical puzzles, stunts, recreations; exhaustively thorough explanations of mathematics involved, analysis of effects, citation of puzzles and games. Mathematics involved is elementary. Translated by F. Göbel. 194 figures. xxiv + 430pp.   22134-2 Paperbound $3.50

Mathematics, Magic and Mystery, Martin Gardner. Puzzle editor for Scientific American explains mathematics behind various mystifying tricks: card tricks, stage "mind reading," coin and match tricks, counting out games, geometric dissections, etc. Probability sets, theory of numbers clearly explained. Also provides more than 400 tricks, guaranteed to work, that you can do. 135 illustrations. xii + 176pp.

20335-2 Paperbound $1.75

MATHEMATICAL PUZZLES FOR BEGINNERS AND ENTHUSIASTS, Geoffrey Mott-Smith. 189 puzzles from easy to difficult—involving arithmetic, logic, algebra, properties of digits, probability, etc.—for enjoyment and mental stimulus. Explanation of mathematical principles behind the puzzles. 135 illustrations. viii + 248pp.
20198-8 Paperbound $1.75

PAPER FOLDING FOR BEGINNERS, William D. Murray and Francis J. Rigney. Basiest book on the market, clearest instructions on making interesting, beautiful origami. Sail boats, cups, roosters, frogs that move legs, bonbon boxes, standing birds, etc. 40 projects; more than 275 diagrams and photographs. 94pp.
20713-7 Paperbound $1.00

TRICKS AND GAMES ON THE POOL TABLE, Fred Herrmann. 79 tricks and games—some solitaires, some for two or more players, some competitive games—to entertain you between formal games. Mystifying shots and throws, unusual caroms, tricks involving such props as cork, coins, a hat, etc. Formerly *Fun on the Pool Table*. 77 figures. 95pp.
21814-7 Paperbound $1.25

HAND SHADOWS TO BE THROWN UPON THE WALL: A SERIES OF NOVEL AND AMUSING FIGURES FORMED BY THE HAND, Henry Bursill. Delightful picturebook from great-grandfather's day shows how to make 18 different hand shadows: a bird that flies, duck that quacks, dog that wags his tail, camel, goose, deer, boy, turtle, etc. Only book of its sort. vi + 33pp. 6½ x 9¼.
21779-5 Paperbound $1.00

WHITTLING AND WOODCARVING, E. J. Tangerman. 18th printing of best book on market. "If you can cut a potato you can carve" toys and puzzles, chains, chessmen, caricatures, masks, frames, woodcut blocks, surface patterns, much more. Information on tools, woods, techniques. Also goes into serious wood sculpture from Middle Ages to present, East and West. 464 photos, figures. x + 293pp.
20965-2 Paperbound $2.00

HISTORY OF PHILOSOPHY, Julián Marías. Possibly the clearest, most easily followed, best planned, most useful one-volume history of philosophy on the market; neither skimpy nor overfull. Full details on system of every major philosopher and dozens of less important thinkers from pre-Socratics up to Existentialism and later. Strong on many European figures usually omitted. Has gone through dozens of editions in Europe. 1966 edition, translated by Stanley Appelbaum and Clarence Strowbridge. xviii + 505pp.
21739-6 Paperbound $3.50

YOGA: A SCIENTIFIC EVALUATION, Kovoor T. Behanan. Scientific but non-technical study of physiological results of yoga exercises; done under auspices of Yale U. Relations to Indian thought, to psychoanalysis, etc. 16 photos. xxiii + 270pp.
20505-3 Paperbound $2.50

Prices subject to change without notice.

Available at your book dealer or write for free catalogue to Dept. GI, Dover Publications, Inc., 180 Varick St., N. Y., N. Y. 10014. Dover publishes more than 150 books each year on science, elementary and advanced mathematics, biology, music, art, literary history, social sciences and other areas.